INFORMATION & COMMUNICATION TECHNOLOGY

GNVQ

Intermediate

UNITS 1 - 3

ISBN 1 84224 028 5

Intermediate Information and Communication Technology GNVQ
Unit 1, 2 and 3
Published by Liberty Hall Ltd

© Copyright Liberty Hall Ltd, 2000

ISBN 1 84224 028 5

A CIP catalogue record for this book is available from the British Library

First edition 2000

All rights reserved

Without limiting the rights under copyright reserved above, **no part of this publication may be photocopied** or reproduced, stored in or introduced into a retrieval system, or transmitted in any form or by any means, electronic, mechanical, photocopying, recording, or otherwise, without prior permission of the above publisher of this book.

Printed by Liberty Hall Ltd

Cover printed by Bishops Printers

Acknowledgements

Window screen images and icons reprinted with permission from Microsoft Corporation
Microsoft, Windows, Word, Access, Excel and Powerpoint are trademarks of Microsoft Corporation in the U.S.A. and other countries
Clipart produced by Corel Corporation, GSP and Alan Goldsmith

The authors

Chris Doolan is a further education lecturer teaching computer programming and information technology at all levels to HND. She has been involved for many years in courses designed for women returning to education.

Bob Hudson taught in further education for fifteen years. He was head of a large department for eight years. He came to education from industry, where he spent eleven years, firstly as a physicist and then as an analyst/programmer. He currently works for Liberty Hall.

John Ayres is a Deputy Head of Department who has worked for twenty years in further education. For the last fifteen years he has been teaching computing at all levels to HND. He has been a BTEC moderator for the last six years.

Liberty Hall Ltd is a publishing company producing books for students of IT, Computing and Business.

Liberty Hall believes that:

- Education is the key to freedom.

- Good education is achieved through good teaching.

- Good teaching is supported by sound educational material.

- Books should be designed for the students.

- Books should be affordable.

Liberty Hall's books are written by good, experienced teachers who share these values.

Contents Page

This Book — 1

Unit 1 Presenting Information — 5

Chapter 1 - Styles of Writing and Presentation — 7

1.1 Introduction — 7
1.2 What Style of Language Should We Use — 9

Chapter 2 - Types of Information and Document Layout — 15

2.1 Introduction — 15
2.2 Types of Document — 16
2.3 Features of Document Layout — 16
2.4 Positioning of Page Items — 19
2.5 Commercial Documents — 20

Chapter 3 - Presentation Techniques — 25

3.1 Introduction — 25
3.2 Templates — 26
3.3 White Space — 26
3.4 Bold and Italic Text — 26
3.5 Tables — 27
3.6 Tabs — 28
3.7 Subscript and Superscript — 29
3.8 Titles and Headings — 29
3.9 Fonts and Sizes — 30
3.10 Alignment — 30
3.11 Upper and Lower Case — 30
3.12 Graphics — 31
3.13 Borders and/or Shading — 32
3.14 Bullet Points and Numbering — 32
3.15 Columns — 33
3.16 Special Symbols — 33
3.17 Contents and Indexes — 33
3.18 Combining Information — 33
3.19 Copying From One Document to Another — 34
Now It's Time to Test Yourself! — 35

Assessment Unit 1 — 37

Unit 2 Handling Information — 39

Chapter 4 - Information Handling — 41

4.1 Data and Information — 41
4.2 The Structure of Information — 42
4.3 Sources of Information — 44
4.4 Finding Information — 46
4.5 Sorting and Searching for Information — 47
4.6 Types of Information — 48

Chapter 5 - Handling Techniques 49

5.1	Databases	49
5.2	Hypertext Databases	49
5.3	Record-Structured Databases	50
5.4	Number-Structured Databases	51

Chapter 6 - Design of Information Handling Systems 53

6.1	Preparing the Design	53
6.2	Implementing the Design	56

Chapter 7 - Database Methods 57

7.1	Database Terms	57
7.2	Database Design	59
7.3	Case Study - North Barchester College	60
7.4	Constructing a Database	60

Chapter 8 - Spreadsheet Methods 65

8.1	Spreadsheet Terms	65
8.2	What-If Testing	68
8.3	Case Study - ComCom Inc	68
8.4	Producing Charts and Line Graphs	72
	Now It's Time to Test Yourself!	73

Assessment Unit 2 75

Unit 3 Hardware and Software 77

Chapter 9 - Hardware 79

9.1	An ICT System	79
9.2	Input Devices	79
9.3	Output Devices	84
9.4	The Central Processing Unit (CPU)	87
9.5	Auxiliary Storage	89
9.6	Backup Storage Devices	92

Chapter 10 - Software 93

10.1	Introduction	93
10.2	The Operating System	94
10.3	Graphics User Interface	95
10.4	Applications Software	96
10.5	Configuring the System	99
10.6	Types of Application Software	101
10.7	Configuring Application Software	104
10.8	Testing the Operating System and the Application Software	105

Chapter 11 - Computer Programming 107

11.1	Computer Programs	107
11.2	HTML Programs	108
11.3	Using a Web Page Publishing Package	109
11.4	Web Page Design	110
11.5	Macro Programming Languages	111
11.6	The Facilities Available for Creating Automated Routines	112
11.7	Using Wizards	114
11.8	Other Automated Routines	115

Now It's Time to Test Yourself! 117

Assessment Unit 3 119

Chapter 12 - Standard Ways of Working 121

12.1	Introduction	121
12.2	Managing Your Work	121
12.3	Keeping Information Secure	124
12.4	Accuracy and Reliability	126
12.5	Organisations and Standard Formats	127
12.6	Working Safely	128

Index 129

This Book

This book has been designed to support students studying for Units 1, 2 and 3 of their Intermediate GNVQ in Information and Communication Technology.

Unit 1 is called **Presenting Information**. The author is Chris Doolan.

Unit 2 is called **Handling Information**. The author is Bob Hudson.

Unit 3 is called **Hardware and Software**. The author is John Ayres.

What is GNVQ?

GNVQ stands for General National Vocational Qualification and you can see from its name that it has a number of qualities.

It is General in that it provides a broad range of skills that allow a pupil or student to progress in a wide range of career directions.

It is National in that it is running in schools and colleges across England and Wales.

It is Vocational in that it provides knowledge and skills suitable for a wide range of working environments or for entry to University and then to employment.

The body that controls GNVQ is the

Qualifications and Curriculum Authority, the **QCA**.

GNVQs are offered by three awarding bodies which are

The Business and Technology Education Council known as **BTEC** which is part

of the **Foundation for Educational Excellence** known as **Edexcel**

The City and Guilds of London known as **C&G** which is part of

the **Assessment and Qualifications Alliance** known as **AQA**, and

The Royal Society of Arts known as **RSA** which is part of the **OCR** examining

body.

GNVQs provide the same level of qualification as A levels. One GNVQ at Advanced level is equivalent to two A levels.

Why Study for a GNVQ?

GNVQs are quite different from traditional A levels and GCSEs, although some A levels and most GCSEs do have some of the features of GNVQ. They are new and have the advantage of being able to adopt in their design many of the new ideas in education.

What are these ideas?

They are Not Time Constrained

First of all they do not rely on two years of study completed by a set of make-or-break examinations. GNVQs, like many GCSEs and some A levels, have a strong emphasis on continual assessment and allow pupils and students to build up their qualification gradually over a period of time. GNVQs do not have to be completed in one or two years although schools and colleges are likely to offer them to most students over one, two or three years. Increasingly, however, GNVQs are offered over a time period that suits the student. Part-time students in particular would wish to take advantage of this.

They are Modular

Traditional courses run usually for one or two years and usually have an examination or set of examinations at the end. It is not possible to get part of a qualification for doing part of the course. If a student drops out it usually will mean repeating the course.

Modern courses are more student friendly. They try to give the student recognition for achievement throughout the course. This is done by breaking up the course into sections and allowing the student to gain a credit for each section successfully completed. These sections are sometimes called **modules**. In GNVQ programmes the term **units** is used instead of **modules**. GNVQ courses are called **programmes**.

They are Skills-based

Traditional courses tried to test knowledge by examination through questioning and it was often the case that the questions confused the students. GNVQs try to test knowledge by examining the skills that the student has gained as well as limited questioning. GNVQs, therefore, are considered to be activity based and practical rather than purely academic.

How Does it Work?

Units

As stated above GNVQ programmes are divided into units. In the advanced programmes there are twelve vocational units and in the intermediate programmes there are six vocational units. Some units are **mandatory** in that they have to be completed successfully by the student to get the qualification and the rest are **optional** in that a pupil or student can choose which units to study to complete the programme.

$$\boxed{\text{GNVQ}} = \boxed{\text{MANDATORY}} + \boxed{\text{OPTIONAL}}$$

BTEC, C&G and RSA offer the same mandatory units but different optional units, except at Foundation level.

The Advanced GNVQ has six mandatory vocational units and six optional vocational units while the Intermediate GNVQ has three mandatory vocational units and three optional vocational units.

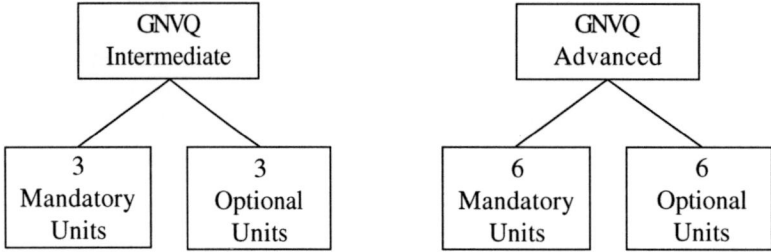

In addition there are three GNVQ **compulsory or mandatory** key skills units. These are:

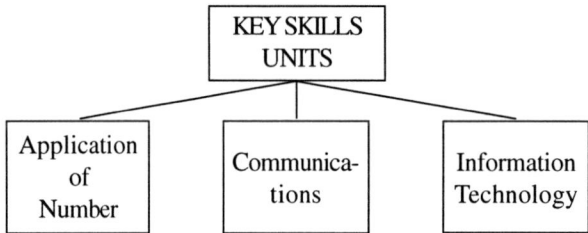

Part One GNVQ

Part One GNVQ is offered at two levels:

Intermediate level, which is equivalent to two GCSE's at grades A to C. For this you must pass Units 1,2 and 3 of GNVQ Intermediate Level in Information and Communication Technology.

Foundation level, which is equivalent to two GCSE's at grades D to G. For this you must pass Units 1,2 and 3 of GNVQ Foundation Level in Information and Communication Technology.

Advanced GNVQ - the Six Unit Award and the Three Unit Award

From September 2000, the Advanced GNVQ will be offered as six unit awards. A six unit award will be equivalent to one A level.

There will also be a three unit award. For this you must pass Units 1,2 and 3 of GNVQ Advanced Level in Information and Communication Technology.

Unit 1 Presenting Information
by Chris Doolan

This unit is called **Presenting Information**.

It will help you to:

- write original documents in **styles** that suit your readers
- improve the **accuracy and readability** of the documents you create
- improve the **quality of presentation** in documents you create
- choose and apply **standard document layouts**
- understand and develop **good practice** in your use of ICT

You will create and compose a variety of documents using layout and styles that suit their different purposes. You will compare the style and layout of documents that you create with similar documents produced by organisations.

This unit links closely with Unit 2: Handling Information and will be assessed only through an external assessment. The grade for that assessment will be your grade for the unit.

Key skills

When you complete the work in this unit, you will have the opportunity to satisfy the following key skills components.

Application of number, level 2

When you are:	You will have the oportunity to develop the following key skills evidence:
using charts, graphs and tables	N2.3 Interpret the results of your calculations and present your findings. You must use at least one graph, one chart and one diagram.

Communication, level 2

When you are:	You will have the opportunity to develop the following key skills evidence:
choosing and using appropriate writing styles and layouts	C2.3 Write two different types of documents about straightforward subjects. One piece of writing should be an extended document and include at least one image.
using standard ways of working	

Chapter 1
Styles of Writing and Presentation

Objectives

At the end of this chapter you will be able to describe

- styles of writing
- styles of language

1.1 Introduction

This unit is concerned with communication using different styles and presentation techniques to satisfy the needs of the user. You will be expected to create a number of documents with different styles. The style that you use will depend on the purpose of the document. The purposes considered in this chapter are:

meeting the needs of your reader
attracting attention
setting out facts clearly
explaining details
summarising information

A   Meeting the Needs of Your Reader

You will see how the style of writing varies depending on the person or people we need to communicate with. The whole point of communication is to get a message across; the type of reader will determine the style of correspondence. Remember that too much information is almost as bad at too little. It is very irritating to have to read through an entire huge report in order to extract just one or two points that concern the reader. The presentation and the language in which the document is written will need to change to meet the needs of the reader.

B   Attracting attention

If a reader finds a communication difficult to understand then the aim of the correspondence has not been achieved. The need to attract attention is important, and for some purposes can be absolutely vital. Imagine that you need to design a sign giving instructions on what to do in the case of an emergency; the style would be very different from that of a business letter or memo. It must really 'grab' the readers' attention. Bold colours and text are required and instructions should be clear and concise.

C Setting out facts clearly

Unlike letters which you write to friends, it is important to get your message across in a factual manner. Don't stray from the point and don't use 'flowery' language. Always finish one topic before starting on another. In business people have little time to read correspondence and so all communications should come to the point as quickly as possible and the language used should leave no room for error. Both parties should be in no doubt as to the meaning and purpose of the correspondence.

Each new fact should have a paragraph to itself. When making lists you might like to indent slightly and bullet mark them. You may either set your own indentation or simply press the indent (Tab) key once.

Tab key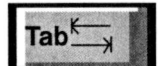

- You have a choice of bullet marks and these can be viewed and, in Microsoft Word 2000, selected by clicking on **Format** from the toolbar and then clicking on **Bullets and Numbering**. If you decide the type of bullet you have used is not right, simply highlight the whole bulleted points and re-select, using the same process.

2   The need to set out facts clearly in reports is essential. Some reports can run to dozens of pages. You must find a means to identify facts in greater depth than simply using a bullet, this is done by **numbering paragraphs**. Each main paragraph or topic will have a number and if you then want to go into more detail within that paragraph you can give additional numbers to identify 'sub paragraphs'.

This example might be an extract from a report:

2   GENERAL METHODS USED

    2.1   QUESTIONNAIRES

        2.1.1   CLOSED QUESTIONNAIRES

        2.1.2   OPEN QUESTIONNAIRES

This may seem a little unnecessary until you imagine how both parties will discuss a very lengthy report if there are a number of queries. It is much simpler if the recipient can say: 'I have a query on point 2.1.2 of your report', rather than: 'I have a query on page 17 of your report. It's about halfway down the page. It's the sentence beginning ……..'.

D Explaining details

When you are writing correspondence it is easy to forget that the recipient may not understand what you are trying to say. You may be very familiar with the subject and take it for granted that the reader is also just as knowledgeable. You should never use technical language unless it is appropriate to the reader.

E Summarising information

The need to summarise information is very important. Quite often the reader will read the summary first so that he/she knows the main points contained within the correspondence. From the writer's point of view it is always a good idea to summarise facts as it will ensure that everything has been covered. When writing reports you must always give a detailed summary; with letters, unless quite lengthy, it is less important.

1.2 What Style of Language Should We Use?

When writing to a young child you must obviously keep the language as simple as possible. The sentences should be short and plenty of space should be allowed between paragraphs, as young children may be put off by large blocks of text. Where possible pictures/graphics should be inserted to keep their interest.

When writing to friends you may write in a relaxed way. The rules that relate to business letters do not apply to personal correspondence. If you suddenly changed your style of writing they might think you had become pompous!

Business letters, reports etc., need to be formal. You should ensure that your grammar and spelling are correct and, thanks to word processing software which allows for grammar and spelling checks, life has never been easier!

Example 1   Business Correspondence

Never begin a letter by saying: 'I am writing ....'. They know you are writing to them; they have the letter in front of them!

Never say 'a lot'. What does this mean? Your idea of 'a lot', will differ from the reader's. Be specific. Example: not 'a lot of the monitors you sent us were faulty' but '5 of the monitors you sent us were faulty'. You would then go on to describe the nature of the fault.

If when writing to a Company, you have a contact name, then use it, e.g.

Mr T G Sharpe
Sales Department
Smart Software Limited
Silicon House
North Street
Chichester
West Sussex
PO19 8JJ

Dear Mr Sharpe

xxxxxx xxxx xxxxxxx xxxxx xxxxxxxxxx xxxx xxxxxxxxx xxxxx xxxxxx
xxx xxxx xx xx xxxx xxxxx xxxx xxxxx xxx xxx xxxxxx xxxxx xxxxx xxxxx xxx

Yours sincerely

A N Other
Purchasing Director
Smith & Jones Limited

If you do not have a contact name:

Smart Software Limited
Silicon House
North Street
Chichester
West Sussex
PO19 8JJ

Dear Sirs

xxxxx xxxxx xx xxxxx xxxxxx x xxx xxxx xxxxxxx xxx xxxxx xxx xxxx xxx
xxx xxxxx xxx xxxx xx xxxxx xxxx xxx xxxxxxx xxxxx xxx xxxxx xxxx xx

Yours faithfully

A N Other
Purchasing Director
Smith & Jones Limited

Note: **Yours sincerely** when the contact name is known but **Yours faithfully** when the contact name is not known.

You must acquire good letter writing skills. Letters may be your only point of contact and they must be impressive.

Example 2   Job Application

The quality, layout and content of your letter of application, your curriculum vitae and possibly a completed application form, will either get you to an interview or not. It doesn't matter how well you come across when speaking to somebody, you may have bags of charm and charisma, but unless you can write a good letter you will never have the chance to demonstrate how good you are.

Example 3   A letter to a newspaper

In order that the newspaper may print a letter, it must have 'reader appeal' and the language should be 'punchy' enough to grab the readers' attention. Newspaper Editors enjoy controversial subjects, and so people who write with very definite opinions, are more likely to see their letter in print. Look in some daily newspapers and see the different styles of readers' letters selected for inclusion.

They are normally 'open' letters, i.e. not aimed at one person, but at readers in general. Some letters to newspapers can be quite humorous, and instead of the writer's name, the letter may be 'signed' as 'Disgusted of Midhurst', or 'Perplexed of Petersfield'.

Let's look at some more examples of correspondence:

Example 4   A Formal Letter Responding to a Job Advertisement

This must be carefully set out and written. Ensure that your address appears at the top of the page, either on the right or left-hand side of the page. The Company's name and address comes next and should be on the left-hand side of the page. If the advertisement gives a contact name you must use this. Sometimes you will notice that a job reference is given in the advertisement and you should type this in your letter. The current date, in the correct format, should appear before you begin the main body of the letter, e.g. 22 May 2000.

Your letter should include:

the name of the publication where you saw the job advertised and
the title of the position.
If you are requesting a job application form, then say so.
If you have already received and completed the application form, then state that the completed form is enclosed.
If you are sending a copy of your C V (curriculum vitae), you should mention the fact.
State the reasons why you feel you are suitable for the post advertised.

Example 5   Drawing up an Agenda for a Meeting

Agendas should be businesslike, brief and to the point, but you must get the message across.
When will the meeting take place and where?
Who will be attending the meeting?
What points will be discussed?

The first item on an agenda will be the reading of the minutes of the last meeting. Further items for discussions may or may not have been agreed at the previous meeting. Agendas should be sent early, allowing plenty of time for everybody attending the meeting to have had a chance to examine each topic, in order that they can make a useful contribution to the meeting.

The final item on the agenda is always any other business, referred to as AOB. Allowance for any other business is necessary as the meeting may well generate problems in areas which had not previously been considered.

An example is:

The Rubber Bottomed Coracle Committee

The next meeting of the committee will take place at Saddler's Lodge, at 7.30 pm on Tuesday the 19th May 1999. The meeting will discuss the following items.

1. The repair to our coracle fleet.

2. Barney's boots.

3. The Christmas party.

4. Any other business.

The meeting will end at 9.00 pm.

Example 6   Minutes of a Meeting

There is a definite art to taking minutes of a meeting. The person responsible for minute taking must begin by making a note of everybody present. Anybody on the original list who has not attended should be noted. They must listen very carefully and make a note of all the points made and who made them. Meetings unfortunately do not always run smoothly and you might well find that somebody starts talking about a topic already covered; so you must make a note of where to insert the new points raised.

The minute taker must use his/her judgement of when to omit items. For example, it is not a good idea to include any unpleasant personal remarks which may have been made. If in doubt about what to include, the chairperson of the meeting should be consulted before the minutes are written and distributed.

It is necessary to ensure that the minutes are correctly titled and the distribution list is printed on the front page of the minutes. Example:

MINUTES OF MONTHLY SALES MEETING
10:30 HRS ~ 11 MAY 2000

Chairperson: Daniel Stewart
Present: DB, PC, JD, MF, PP, DS, MT, RW
Apologies: MM   (*Denotes this person was unable to attend*)

Each fact mentioned during the meeting must appear in the minutes and it is normal to add the name or initials of the person making the point, e.g.

JD stated that the system of backing up files should be investigated as it had been noted that not all departments were taking regular back-ups and as a result some loss of data had occurred.

Example 7   Writing an advertisement

The style of writing and presenting an advertisement will depend on what and how you propose to sell an item. A simple advertisement to be placed in a local newspaper will be very different from an advertisement in a glossy magazine.

This is fine for a simple advertisement but an advertisement for a glossy magazine requires far more thought. For example, if it were necessary to write an advertisement to launch a new range of cosmetics, you would need to think about the audience you wanted to reach. Very expensive cosmetics will normally be advertised in more exclusive magazines. The age of the target group must also be borne in mind, as the type of magazine read will often be dependent on the age of the reader.

> Mountain bike suit 7-9 yr old.
> VGC £50 ONO.
> (01435) 812218 evening only.

Note that the advertising is very brief and to the point. Abbreviations are often used, e.g. VGC.

Such advertisements should not be too wordy; graphics and/or photographs are eye catching and likely to prove more attractive than paragraphs of text. In order to highlight the type of cosmetic being advertised, an appropriate photograph must be used, e.g. lips for lipstick, eyes for mascara, eye shadow, eyebrow pencil, etc. The brand name of the cosmetic must be prominently displayed and, if the company has a logo, this too will help the reader to recognise the brand.

Example 8   Writing a note to the milkman

As with the advertisement, the note is very informal and to the point, e.g. '**1 extra litre today please**'. If the note is placed inside an empty milk bottle on your doorstep, you don't even need to give your name and address.

Example 9   A formal invitation to a social event

Formal invitations are normally printed on card. They will often have a decorative border and the lettering may be in gold or silver and the font style will often be very stylish. One example of a formal invitation to a social event is an invitation to a wedding. When the wording of the invitation has been decided upon, the style of card will be chosen and the invitations specially printed. The invitation will bear the name of the bride's parents, the name of the prospective bride and groom and details relating to the wedding and/or the wedding reception, i.e. place, date and time. RSVP will be printed on the invitation and this means a response to the invitation is required.

Example 10   Tables

Tables are often used as a means of showing results. In order that the table makes sense to the reader, it is necessary that suitable headings be used. For example, if you wished to show football clubs' positions in a particular league, you would make a main heading to show what the table conveyed. Other headings required would be the name of the club, the points accumulated to date and the number of games played.

Example 11   Forms

A large number of different forms are used in business including purchase orders, invoices etc. Most organisations, and indeed many homes, own fax machines and so a form for a fax header page will also need to be designed.

Activity 1.1

1. Produce a formal letter to a business using a word processor, asking for information about one of their products.

Activity 1.2

1. Use a word processor to produce an advertisement for your car that you could place in the local newspaper. Use text only and no more than 20 words.

2. Re-create your advert to fit a quarter page box. Add graphics, enlarge text, use different font styles and sizes. If you have a coulour printer, add colour.

Activity 1.3

1. Create a company name and a logo.

2. Use a word processor to produce a business letter, a memo and a business card using the name and logo.

Print all the documents produced in the activities above.

Chapter 2
Types of Information and Document Layout

Objectives

At the end of this chapter you should be able to describe

- types of information
- types of document
- features of document layout
- positioning of page items
- commercial documents

2.1 Introduction

Whatever the style or type of communication, the end result is always the same, it is to convey and share information. There are different types of information and information from one source will often be combined with information from another source in order to build up a complete picture.

For example, you may be writing a report using a word processing package. At some point it is likely that you will wish to clarify a point made by inserting a table, columns from a spreadsheet, graph or other form of graphic. When inserting such details their style must be made to conform to the style used in the report. If the report is well constructed, the reader should not be aware that such inserts do not form a natural part of the report. Later on we will look at how this can best be achieved.

When you produce your documents, you should be able to include different types of information including:

Text   e.g.   Font Types - Arial   Font sizes - 8 point

Italics   **Bold**   <u>Underline</u>

Numbers

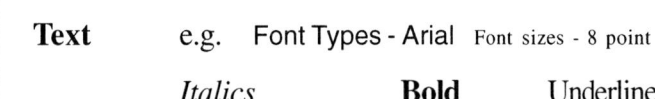

Tables	Brown	£23,000	£32,000	£18,500
	Green	£45,000	£48,500	£34,000
	Grey	£22,000	£30,000	£28,000

Graphs and Charts

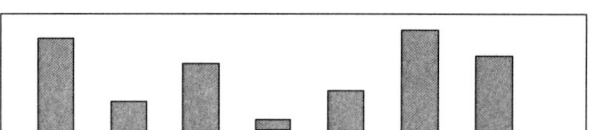

Graphics

2.2 Types of Document

The following is just a brief example of different types of document with different layouts:

Memos ~ a memorandum or memo is normally quite informal and is written and circulated internally, **within** a company.

Business letters ~ formal letters are written and sent externally, outside the organisation.

Reports ~ formal and informal reports are written. Such reports may be for internal or external use.

Agendas and Minutes of Meetings are normally for internal use but can also be external.

Newsletters are informative and often circulated to members of a club or possibly employees of the company. They should be informative and eye catching.

Screen displays, either for use on a computer's monitor or a display panel, should be clearly set out so that the viewer understands the meaning of the display and can act on instructions if given.

Publicity flyers are a cheap means of advertising.

Business cards ~ business cards may be handed out in order to make contacts and they will bear the name of the person, their position within the organisation, and details of the organisation (name and address, etc).

Itineraries ~ a list of events and/or places in the order in which they occur. For example, if you are planning a holiday you may draw up an itinerary with dates and contact numbers to leave with friends and/or work mates.

2.3 Features of Document Layout

Once the type and design of the form has been decided upon, the actual layout must be considered. Such decisions will include:

A   Paper size and orientation.

Very small pieces of paper are not a good idea since they may get lost. On the other hand it is unlikely that you would use A3 size paper for general correspondence. The orientation of the paper will normally be portrait rather than landscape, although there may be some exceptions.

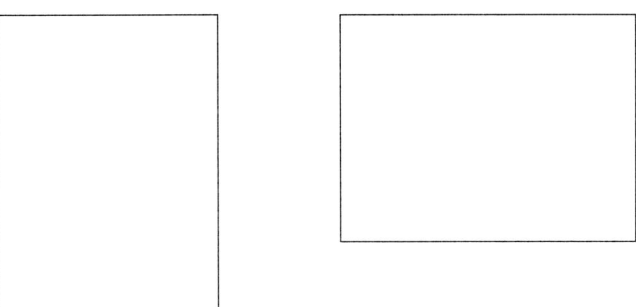

Portrait   **Landscape**

B   Paragraph Format

You may decide whether you wish to indent the first line of your paragraphs, leave them in block form or you may like to see hanging paragraphs. Example:

> This is an example of an indent paragraph – 1.5" left indent. You will notice that the paragraph forms a block which is all indented, i.e. each line of the paragraph begins at the same margin.

This is an example of a 'first line' layout. You will see that if we continue to type for more than one line, the second and subsequent lines go back to the margin.

This is an example of a hanging paragraph. If we continue to type for more than one line you will see that only the first line is against the margins, the others 'hang' from the first line.

C   Margins

The margin is the distance from the edge of the page (left, right, top and bottom). You may set margins

either by selecting the Format choice from the main toolbar for margins within a paragraph

or by moving the cursor onto the existing margin on the ruler bar, holding down the button and dragging it to the point required before releasing the button.

The four margins are shown below

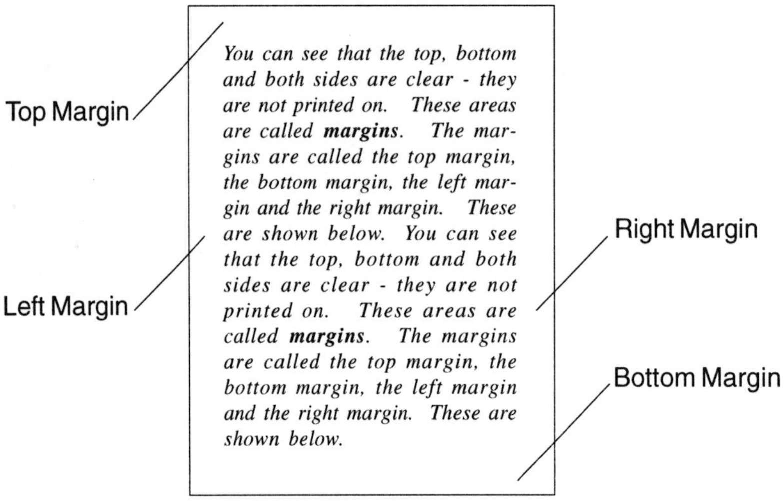

Top Margin

Left Margin

*You can see that the top, bottom and both sides are clear - they are not printed on. These areas are called **margins**. The margins are called the top margin, the bottom margin, the left margin and the right margin. These are shown below. You can see that the top, bottom and both sides are clear - they are not printed on. These areas are called **margins**. The margins are called the top margin, the bottom margin, the left margin and the right margin. These are shown below.*

Right Margin

Bottom Margin

D   Headers and Footers

These are a good means of identifying the piece of work. There are various styles of headers and footers. As the names suggest, the header will appear at the top of the page and the footer at the bottom of the page. We will look at them now and think of the type of things we might like to include:

Select **View** from the main toolbar.
Now select **Header and Footer**
A new header and footer toolbar will appear which will allow you to make style choices. You will also notice that a box appears with the word 'header' and you may simply type in your header. You may choose a different style and size of font if you wish.

E.g.

Liberty Hall Ltd - Header

Liberty Hall Ltd - Footer

To see the various options on the special toolbar simply move the cursor to each of the options and a written description will appear.

When you have completed your header you can design your footer. To allow you to insert text for the footer you must select 'switch between header and footer' on the special tool bar. When you have added your footer you simply select 'close' from the toolbar.

What things could you include in your footer? You might like to insert the name of the person responsible for compiling the sales report, you might insert page numbering and you might like to include the distribution date of the report. There are lots of options so practice using headers and footers until you feel confident.

E   Line spacing

If you are writing letters, reports, etc., it is normal for single line spacing to be used and this is always the default setting, i.e. unless you change the spacing it will always remain the same. If you need to write a draft of a letter or report it is normal to use double line spacing. This allows for editing. The reader can add, change or delete lines of the draft document, as there is space enough to do so. The word processor operator can then take the amended draft letter or report and make corrections until, when the work is finally agreed, he/she can revert back to single line spacing before saving and printing the document.

F   Fonts

The number of fonts available will depend on the software which has been installed on the computer. Years ago the number of fonts available on computers was quite limited but now there are a huge amount of styles from which to choose.

To see the full extent of the fonts available, position the cursor on the down arrow beside the default font box on the tool bar and use the mouse to scroll down the list. Try out various fonts, some of them have surprising results!

Business letters, reports, memos etc., should be completed in fairly conventional fonts as they are easy to read. Times New Roman and Arial are commonly used for such purposes. If you wanted something more eye-catching you would select a more stylish font and possibly increase the size and colour.

2.4 Positioning of Page Items

There is no set, standard page layout for documents. Try looking at letters received in your own home. Many years ago typists would always be told to adhere to set rules for positioning items on a page. Now, however, companies decide for themselves, what and where things should appear in their correspondence.

Let's look at things to be included:

Logos
Headings
References
Dates
Addressee names
Signatures

2.5 Commercial Documents

Commercial organisations use many documents. These include business letters, memoranda, reports, newsletters, invoices, minutes and agendas. In order to project the image of their organisation they develop a **corporate style**. This is achieved by creating all their documents with the same style and layout and using the same company logo or trade mark on each. This is also called a **house style**. In fact, it is more likely to be the logo that is recognised by the public. This means that when a member of the public or a customer sees a document, they know from its style which organisation has produced it. If you look around you, you will see many examples of this. The Virgin range of companies uses a written version of their name on all its materials and advertisements and is instantly recognised by the public. Tesco and Sainsbury have names that are recognised by style as do many other high street shops.

A corporate style is chosen to ensure that information is simply presented and creates an image that provides good publicity.

Organisations like to project a recognisable corporate image to the public and like to win loyalty from the public for their goods and services. They aim for their name and logo to be associated with their goods and services.

The documents that will project the corporate image are described as follows:

A   Business Letter

In businesses, letters are usually written on headed stationery. A letter will include a **Ref**erence, a **Date**, an **Addressee/Address**, a **Letter Heading**, the **Body** of the letter, a **Complimentary Close** and **Enclosures** (if needed). An example is shown below.

The Bookworm Bookstore
High Street
Bichester
Hants
HB20 6DC

Ref: th/ds/89

1st May 1997

Mr I Readalot
1 Blacksmiths Cottages
Bichester
Hants

Dear Mr Readalot

'Fly Fishing' by J R Hartley

We are pleased to inform you that your order of 'Fly Fishing' by J R Hartley has arrived. You can collect it between 9.00 am and 5.30 pm Monday to Saturday.

Yours sincereley

Mr I Readeven-More
Manager

B   Memorandum

A memorandum, memo for short, is used for **internal communication.** It is usually **brief**, but could be lengthy. It will include the **Date**, **From** whom sent, **To** whom sent, a **Ref**erence and the **Subject** of the memorandum. There is no need for a salutation or a complementary close such as *Yours sincerely*. An example is shown below.

MEMORANDUM

TO: Mr I Readeven-More

FROM: Miss Takes

DATE: 15th April 1997

REF: th/25

SUBJECT: Book Order ds/89 'Fly Fishing' by J R Hartley

Please note the above book has now been ordered. According to the publishers delivery will be approximately 2 weeks.

C   Report

These are of two types, the Informal Report which includes Introduction, Information and Conclusions, and the Formal Report which includes Terms of Reference, Procedures, Findings, Conclusions and Recommendations.

D   Newsletter

A newsletter is a collection of news items relating to an organisation. It might have one page or it might have many. The newsletter might be sent to all its customers informing them of new products or it might be a newsletter sent to staff telling them about their organisation.

E   Agenda

This is a list of the items to be discussed at a meeting and is sent to all those who are to attend the meeting.

AGENDA

Participants: Mr I Readeven-More, Miss Takes, Mr M Ployed

Date: 20th April 1997

Venue: Staff Room

Time: 10.00 am

1. Discuss last months book sales
2. New price rises
3. Holidays for next year

F Minutes

Minutes are a record of who attends a meeting and what decisions are made at it. Minutes include the **Specifics of a Meeting** particularly decisions, **Those Present, Apologies for Absence, Matters Arising** from previous meetings and **Any Other Business** not listed on the agenda. There is an **Action Column** which specifies who is to take action on each item in the minutes.

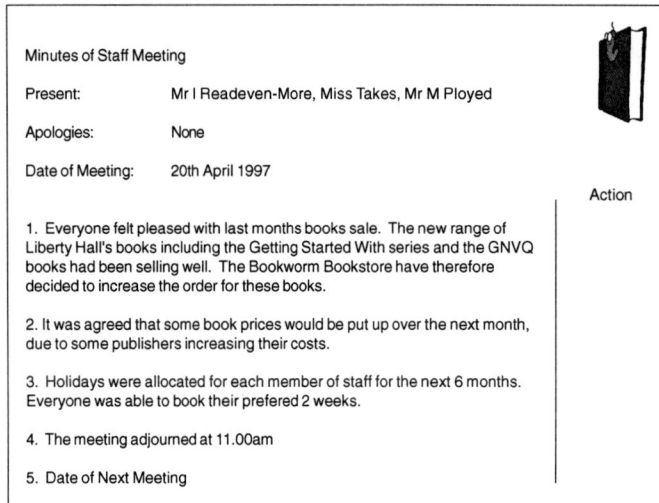

G Sales and Purchasing Documents

These are documents that are used by businesses when dealing with their customers and suppliers. These include Purchase Orders, Sales Orders, Delivery Notes, Sales Invoices and Purchase Invoices.

Order An order for goods or services is made using an order form. The order form will have a unique order number and will hold the details of the customer and the details of the goods or services ordered. These will include the Stock Number, Description, Quantity and Price of the ordered items. A **sales order** is an order from a customer for goods or services. A **purchase order** is an order to a supplier for goods and services.

Delivery Note A delivery note is a document that accompanies goods when they are being delivered. The customer signs the delivery note when the goods are received and the delivery note is taken back to the accounts department of the supplier. The delivery note will contain the customer's order number, the Stock Number, the Description and the Quantity but not Price.

Invoice When the goods or services have been delivered, an invoice will be sent by the supplier to the customer showing the amount to be paid. The invoice will contain the customer's order number, the Stock Number, the Description, the Quantity, the Total, the VAT and the Grand Total. A **sales invoice** is the invoice that a supplier sends to its customer and a **purchase invoice** is one that a customer receives from its supplier.

To help ensure a corporate image, **templates** are used for the above documents. A template is an electronic file which holds an **outline** document image which includes the style and layout that the organisation wants. Other data can be added and displayed before the document is printed.

An example of an order form is shown below.

```
                        ORDER FORM

                     MILLY, MOLLY MANDY
                       11 Grove Road
                         RYEBANK
                         RY2 6PE
                     TEL: 01292 142536
                     FAX: 01292 145789

ORDER NO:  896                                      DATE: 03/04/00

Supplier:
NICK'S METALWORKS
5 Ryebank Industrial Estate
Aden Close
RY21 4TU
```

Stock Number	Description	Quantity	Price per item
MS323	Metal Screws	300 Packs	£1.00

Signature _ _ _ _ _ _ _ _ _ _ _ _

A corresponding delivery note is:

```
                       DELIVERY NOTE
                          NO:789

                     NICK'S METALWORKS
                  5 Ryebank Industrial Estate
                         Aden Close
                          RY21 4TU
                     TEL: (01342) 839702
                      FAX: 1234 939702

ORDER NO:  896                                       DATE:10/04/00

MILLY, MOLLY MANDY
11 Grove Road
RYEBANK
RY2 6PE
```

Stock Number	Description	Quantity
MS323	Metal Screws	300 Packs

Signature _ _ _ _ _ _ _ _   Date _ _ _ _ _ _ _ _

An invoice for the same company is:

INVOICE NO: 789

NICK'S METALWORKS
5 Ryebank Industrial Estate
Aden Close
RY21 4TU
TEL: (01342) 839702
FAX: 1234 939702

ORDER NO: 896   DATE: 10/04/00

MILLY, MOLLY MANDY
11 Grove Road
RYEBANK
RY2 6PE

Stock Number	Description	Quantity	Price per item	Total Cost
MS323	Metal Screws	300 Packs	£1.00	£300.00
			TOTAL	£300.00

Signature __ __ __ __ __ __ __ __ __ __ __ __

Activity 2.1

1. Create an invoice and order form for a company using the company name and logo produced in Activity 1.3

Chapter 3
Presentation Techniques

Objectives

At the end of this chapter you will be able to describe

- design features used to create documents
- copying from one document to another

3.1 Introduction

Thanks to computer software we now have many design tools at our disposal and there should be no excuse for anybody to produce correspondence which is not of an excellent, commercial standard.

Remember ~ computer's don't bite, and providing you save your work regularly, you can experiment as much as you like, without losing your original documents. You won't always get it right the first time; the tendency is to go a little 'over the top' when you begin; the secret is to make your work eye-catching but not gaudy!

Some of the design features available to you are:

Layout grids
Templates
Use of white space
Titles and headings
Fonts and sizes
Bold and italic text
Hanging indents
Tables and tabs
Upper and lower case
Subscript and superscript
Graphics
Colour
Borders and shading
Dividing lines (rules)
Bulleted lists
Justification
Columns
Special symbols
Headers and footers
Charts and graphs
Contents and indexes

We will see how and where to find many of these design options. To describe how to find them all would be too time consuming. You should get used to using the Help from the main toolbar. Now try Contents and Index, then select Index. Type in the topic you wish to search for; then select display. Clear instructions will then appear and you will have the option of printing these instructions if you so wish.

3.2 Templates

For examples to see what **templates** Microsoft Word has to offer, click on **Tools**, then **Templates** and **Add-Ins**, then **Attach**, and a list of available templates will appear ready for your selection.

An example of a letter template is shown below.

[CLICK **HERE** AND TYPE COMPANY NAME]

February 14, 1999

[Click **here** and type recipient's address]

Dear Sir or Madam:

Type your letter here. For more details on modifying this letter template, double-click ✉. To return to this letter, use the Window menu.

Sincerely,

[Click **here** and type your name]
[Click **here** and type job title]

When the template has been loaded, you can key in the text for your letter.

3.3 White Space

We have already talked about the importance of **'white space'** when the document is aimed at a young child. The same is true of us all. There is nothing more off-putting than being faced with great blocks of unbroken text. Some clear white space between paragraphs, or even better an illustration of some sort is far more appealing.

3.4 Bold and Italic Text

To allow for **bold and italic text and underlining** you should either select:

B *I* U

B for bold, *I* for italics or U for underlining from the toolbar, **BEFORE** you type the text or, highlight the text by holding down the left hand mouse button and moving the 'ball' until the text is highlighted, **then** selecting the option of bold, italic or underlining you require. Underlining of headings used to be very popular but is not used very much now as it is thought that emboldened print is more effective.

3.5 Tables

Using **tables and tabs** is necessary when you need to line up text under headings for example. We will begin by looking at tables:

Click on **Table** from the main toolbar
Click on **Insert Table**.
Now select the number of columns and rows
You may leave the column width at auto or select your own size. The 'auto' choice is normally perfectly acceptable and means that you won't have to do any calculations of your own!

If we select 3 columns and 5 rows, the result looks like this:

You can then type within the table if you wish. You can adjust the size if necessary by holding the cursor on one of the lines, holding down the left button and dragging. You can add either to the number of columns or rows if you wish. The cursor needs to be within the table and by selecting **Table**, once again you will be given choices. Apart from adjusting the size of the columns and increasing/decreasing columns and/or rows, you can merge columns together if you wish.

In the following example, I have merged the three columns in row one together, to allow me to give a heading. This is done by highlighting each of the columns to be merged together, clicking on **Table** from the toolbar, and selecting **Merge**.

I have used centre 'justification' for each of the headings. There are four justification options and these can be found to the right hand side of the **U** option on the toolbar.

For the remaining rows, I have chosen to left justify the first two columns and right justify the third. See if you can see why:

JANUARY 2000 - SALE PRICES		
ITEM	DEPARTMENT	PRICE
Addidas Tracksuit	Sports	£28.99
Levis Jeans	Menswear	£24.99
Revlon Lipsticks	Cosmetics	£8.50

Left alignment is generally neater but when using figures you should choose right justification to ensure that figures are correctly aligned. Example:

Incorrect	Correct
£199,876.99	£199,876.99
£0.22	£0.22
£57.99	£57.99

3.6 Tabs

The tab key is used in order to move across the screen to a position where text or numbers are to be entered, rather than pressing the space bar.

By default tabs are preset at 1.27 cm (0.5") intervals. Once you become practiced at using tabs you will find them convenient and easy to use.

The following instructions should be used when using Microsoft Word:

Select **Format**
Select **Tabs**

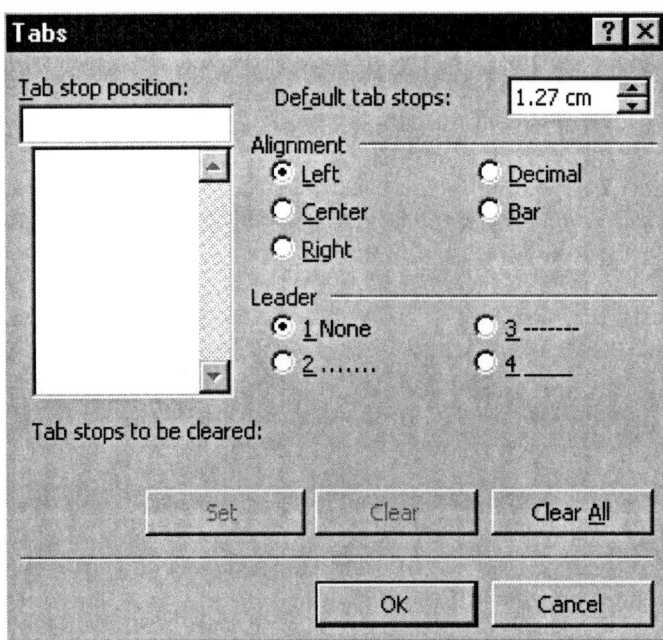

Select **Clear All**
Decide on the position and justification of the first tab stop position and press the 'Set' button.
Continue to set the tabs in the same way and then click **OK**.

Activity 3.1

Try clearing all pre-set tabs and adding new left aligned tabs as follows:
1", 2.2", 3.2", 3.8" - The first title in the table will be typed against the margin.

Ref	Surname	Title	Time	Doctor/Specialist
1234	Smith L	Mr	09:15	Mr Scott
8765	Jones P	Mrs	09:30	Dr Clifford
9765	Dickens J	Mr	10:00	Dr Clifford
7651	Collins W	Mrs	10:15	Mr Scott

Practice using tabs and if one of the columns is to hold currency you should select a 'decimal' tab, as this will align on the decimal point.

3.7 Subscript and Superscript

In the following example,

$$A^2 \;=\; B^2 + C^2$$

the digit 2 is in superscript, i.e. it is raised above the letters.

The following example shows subscripted characters.

$$A_2 \;=\; B_2 + C_2$$

In Word 2000, highlight the character to be subscripted or superscripted, select the **Format** menu, click on **Font**, select the **Font** tab and select the **superscript** or **subscript** box.

3.8 Titles and Headings

Presentation can be improved by using titles and headings. Examples are the chapter headings in this book and the sections heading above.

3.9 Fonts and Sizes

Varying the font and font sizes of the text, the attractiveness of a document can be improved.   It is, however, important not to use too many fonts.

Font   The font is the style of the text used in a document.   Examples are:

Arial

Brooklyn

𝔉𝔯𝔞𝔫𝔨𝔢𝔫𝔰𝔱𝔢𝔦𝔫

PENGUIN

Toronto

Font Size The size of a font is called its point size.   Examples are:

Point 6

Point 9

Point 10

Point 20

Point 35

Point 60

3.10 Alignment

There are four types of text alignment.

Left justified   This is text with its left margin straight and the right margin ragged *This is the default option.*
Centred   This is text with each line centred horizontally.
Right justified   This is text with its left margin ragged and right margin straight. This is not often used.
Fully justified   This is text with both left and right margins straight.

To change alignment click on the desired alignment on the Formatting Tool Bar

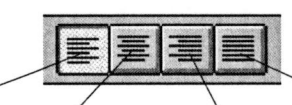

for left justification   for centred text   for right justification   for fully justified text

Examples are

| This piece of text is Left justified. | This piece of text is Centred. | This piece of text is Right justified. | This piece of text is Fully justified. |

3.11 Upper and Lower Case

Text can be presented in **UPPER CASE** or **lower case** or in a mixture such as the title of this section.

3.12   Graphics

Graphics include clip art, pictures, charts and graphs.

Clip Art

To insert a clip art image using Word 2000, select **Picture** from the **Insert** menu and click on **Clip Art**. This will disply the following dialog box.

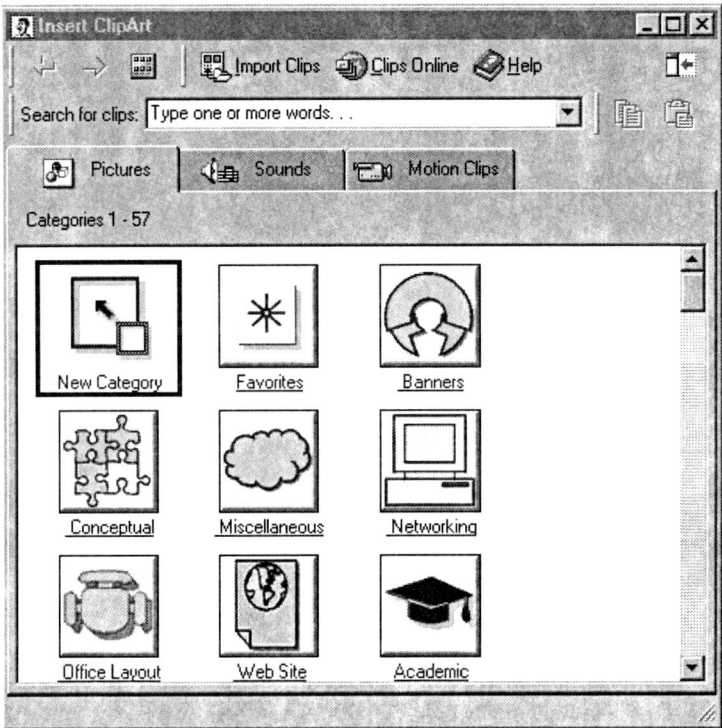

Click on the image that you want to insert and click the insert button displayed.

Charts and Graphs

These can be used from within the word processing software package or from a spreadsheet package. Whether the chart or graph is created from your word processing package or from Microsoft Excel (which forms part of the Microsoft Office suite) it can be easily inserted into any document. A very wide range of choices are available and you should take care to select the most appropriate one to meet your needs. When using charts and graphs it is essential that titles and axis labels are included

Chart

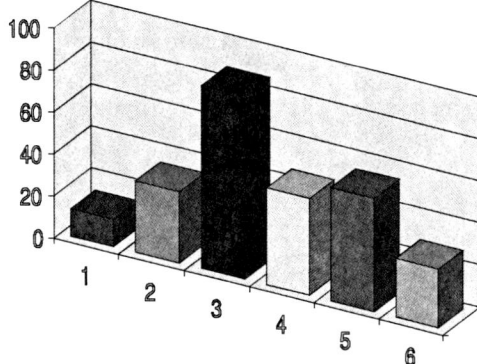

Graph

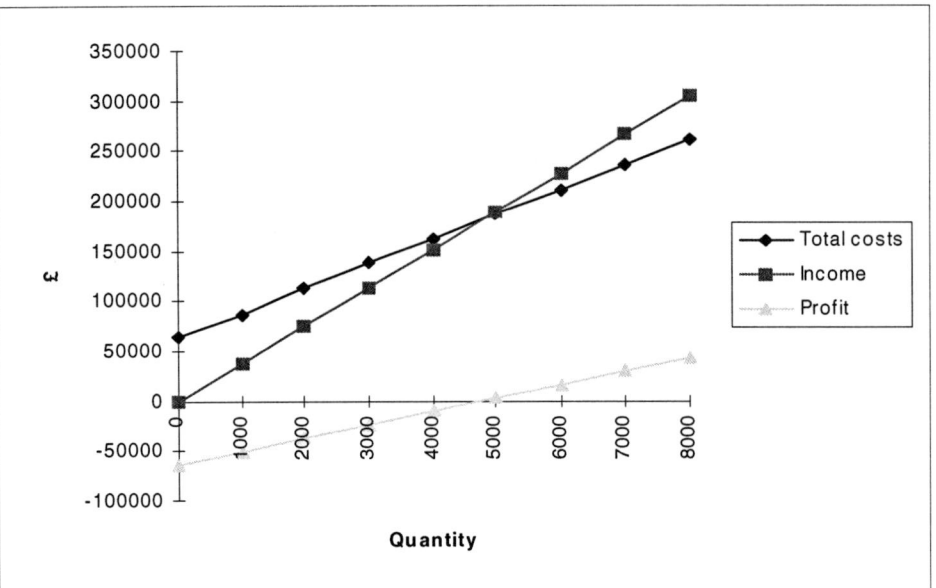

3.13 Borders and/or Shading

Borders and/or shading can be very useful to draw attention to a particular item. To see what Word has to offer, select **Format,** then **Borders and Shading.** You may choose to shade in different colours and different densities. Experiment with as many borders and shading as possible until you fully master the art.

An example of a table with shaded cells and borders is shown below.

	Jan	Feb	Mar
Team A	£345	£456	£418
Team B	£354	£453	£398
Team C	£453	£413	£427
Team D	£436	£398	£421

3.14 Bullet Points and Numbering

Some documents present data in the form of lists. The items in the list can be numbered or can have bullets to emphasise them. For example:

Using bullets   **Using numbers**

Presentation techniques include: Presentation techniques include:

- Margins   1. Margins
- Tables   2. Tables
- Pictures and drawings   3. Pictures and drawings

3.15 Columns

Columns are useful, especially for newsletters etc. To see the options available simply select **Format,** then **Columns.** You may select the size of column and the space between columns. You should select the columns **before** you begin your work and use the **'this point forward'** option to ensure that it does not convert previously entered text which you do not wish to be in columns.

3.16 Special Symbols

Special Symbols are available from the Insert option on the toolbar. You need to select Symbol and then choose either to insert a symbol or special character. Once you have found the symbol you wish to include, simply highlight by pressing the left mouse button and clicking on 'insert'. An example of a symbol is ° to denote degrees.

3.17 Contents and Indexes

Tables of contents and indexes should be used for large documents. The contents page(s) may simply be typed and indexes used for cross-reference purposes. Try looking at 'indexes' from the help index. They can be a little tricky to get used to, but if you follow the instructions from the help menu, the result will be very professional. An example of how indexes work may be that chapter titles can be 'marked' and the software will automatically assign the page number.

3.18 Combining Information

An important requirement of this unit is that you attain a really good grounding in using common software in order to gain the best results.

If you have 'integrated' software such as the Microsoft Office suite, you will see just how easy it is to incorporate text, tables, figures and/or graphics from one package into another. At its simplest you may want to insert a piece of clip art from the word processing package. If you select the Insert option from the toolbar you will see all the options available to you.

If you want to see the range of clip art available, simply select Picture, then Clip Art. A whole range of pictures and possibly some cartoons should be available for you to make your selection. Highlight the one you wish to insert and import the clip you wish. Once on the screen you may change the size or position by using the mouse.

You can insert a whole file/document into another if you wish or a section of that document.

3.19 Copying From One Document to Another

Instructions for cutting and pasting from one file/document to another are:

1. Position the cursor at the point you wish the insert to appear.
2. Open the file holding the section of the document you wish to move.
3. Use the left mouse button to highlight the section you wish to use (you can then either use the **E**dit choice from the toolbar and choose from that menu, or to cut, i.e. remove one section, simply click on the scissors icon on the toolbar).
4. Once you have 'cut' out the piece of text you wish to move it is stored in a buffer area ~ buffer areas are like waiting rooms ~ they hold data waiting to be transferred from one place to another.
5. You may now close the file, which held the text to be moved.
6. Now simply 'paste' from the buffer into your original document.
7. Adjust the newly arrived section if necessary to ensure that the format is identical to the test of the document. This may mean changing margins, font style and size, colour etc.

If you want to 'copy' from one file to another, once the section has been highlighted, instead of clicking on the scissors icon, you click on the 'copy' icon, (appears as two sheets of paper) and then paste as before.

So far we have looked at inserting pictures, text etc., but what if you want to scan in something from another source, e.g. a photograph or text from a magazine etc. Providing you have a scanner with suitable software on your computer, it is very simple.

Once the image has been scanned in, the scanner software will create a file to hold the image and/or text.

To insert the file, simply select **I**nsert from the main menu, then select **Fi**le. Now cursor to the 'Type of File' box and select **All Files**. Now choose the file holding the scanned item and select.

After inserting scanned documents it is essential, especially with text, to read through it thoroughly. Occasionally you will find that the scanning process has 'misread' some letters, possibly due to unusual fonts or poor quality printing. Adjust where necessary and once again ensure that the format of the newly arrived text/picture fits in with the current document.

 Activity 3.2

1. Create a full page advertisement promoting the products of the company for which you produced the name and logo in Activity 1.3. Use some of the techniques described in this chapter. Try to make the advertisement attractive to the reader.

 **Now It's Time to Test Yourself!**

Multiple choice

1. Which of the following is **not** a purpose of writing styles and presentation techniques?

    a. attracting attention
    b. meeting the needs of the reader
    c. choosing the style of an invoice
    d. summarising information

2. Which of the following is an business document?

    a. memorandum
    b. wedding invite
    c. note to a milkman
    d. advertisement

3. Which of the following refers to page orientation?

    a. margin
    b. header
    c. font
    d. portrait

4. A template:

    a. provides a memorandum in italic text
    b. areas of white space in a document
    c. provides the layout of a document
    d. is used for informal documents

5. Tables can be used to:

    a. create charts and graphs
    b. layout information in columns and rows
    c. create templates
    d. create titles and headings

6. Which of the following is a different font style to the rest?

    a. Font   b. Font   c. FONT   d. Font

7. Which of the following is a different font size to the rest?

    a. Font   b. Font   c. FONT   d. Font

8. Which of the following is emphasised text?

    a. underlined   b. emboldened   c. italicised   d. normal

 **Now It's Time to Test Yourself!**

9. Which of the following is bulleted text?

    a. 1. bulleted
        2. bulleted
        3. bulleted

    b. a. bulleted
        b. bulleted
        c. bulleted

    c. i. bulleted
        ii. bulleted
        iii bulleted

    d. • bulleted
        • bulleted
        • bulleted

10. Borders and shading can be applied to:

    a. tabs   b. margins   c. tables   d. alignment

Assessment
Unit 1

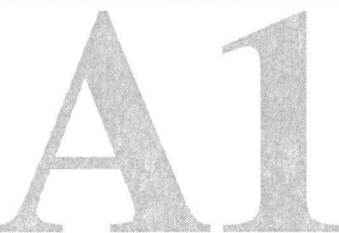

In this unit, you are to produce evidence showing your understanding of documents for different purposes.

These must include:

a range of writing styles and layouts

text created by you and acquired from other sources

structured information in tables

graphics, such as pictures, drawings or clip art.

If you are successful, you will be awarded a Pass, Merit or Distinction according to the following.

Pass

To achieve a Pass your work must show:

P1   your ability to choose and use appropriate writing styles and layouts so that your documents work as intended.

P2   appropriate use of page orientation, paragraph formats, line spacing, headings, margins, headers/footers, tabs, bullets, fonts, borders and shading to enhance your documents.

P3   your ability to originate suitable information and combine it appropriately with different types of material selected from other sources to create combinations of text, pictures, drawings, charts and tables.

P4   your ability to check the accuracy of your work and keep backup copies of all files.

P5   a clear description and comparison of different layouts used by organisations with your own layouts, identifying similarities and differences.

Merit

To achieve a Merit your work must **also** show:

M1   imaginative use of document layouts and presentation techniques to achieve good quality and an appropriate impact in your documents.

M2   your ability to proof-read your work and corrected obvious errors.

M3   relevant explanations for the differences between each of the documents used by different organisations and your own documents.

M4   your ability to work independently to produce your work to agreed deadlines.

M5   your ability to save and annotate draft work to show clearly the development process for two of your documents.

Distinction

To achieve a Distinction your work must **also** show:

D1   different types of information is organised into a convincing and coherent presentation.

D2   information that is accurate and concise and is presented in ways that make it easy to understand.

D3   your ability to use technical language fluently and produce clear, coherent and comprehensive explanations and annotations.

D4   a constructive evaluation of your documents that identifies good and less good features, suggests possible improvements to them and compares them with stand ards used by organisations.

Unit 2 Handling Information
by Bob Hudson

This book has been designed to support students studying for Unit 2 of their Intermediate GNVQ in Information and Communication Technology. This unit is called **Handling Information**.

This unit will help you to:

- understand what **information handling** means and how it is used
- **create a database** to store and process records
- **create a spreadsheet** to store and process numerical information
- **search, sort, explore and predict** information
- discover trends and patterns from numerical information
- understand and develop **good practice** and **standarad ways of working** with ICT

You will produce a relational database and a spreadsheet to meet the needs of users together with notes describing the requirements.

This unit links closely with Unit 1: *Presenting Information* and will be assessed through your portfolio work only. The grade for that assessment will be your grade for the unit.

Key skills

When you complete the work in this unit, you will have the opportunity to satisfy the following key skills components.

Application of number, level 2

When you are:	You will have the oportunity to develop the following key skills evidence:
describing the user needs and the information required	N2.1 Interpret information from two different sources, including material containing a graph producing a design plan and identifying the types of information to be processed.
producing a design plan and identifying the types of information to be processed	N2.2 Carry out calculations to do with: a. amounts and sizes. b. scales and proportion. c. handling statistics. d. using formulae.
using their data-processing skills to predict results and print graphs and reports	N2.3 Interpret the results of your calculations and present your findings. You must use at least one graph, one chart and one diagram.

Communication, level 2

When you are:	You will have the opportunity to develop the following key skills evidence:
communicating clearly the user needs and the reasons for selecting database or spreadsheets	C2.1a Contribute to a discussion about a straightforward subject. C2.1b Give a short talk about a straightforward subject, using an image.
describing the ways in which data is to be processed using the database or spreadsheet methods evaluating their work	C2.2 Read and summarise information from two extended documents about a straightforward subject. One of the documents should include at least one image.
producing their design plans or evaluating their completed work	C2.3 Write two different types of documents about straightforward subjects. One piece of writing should be an extended document and include at least one image.

Chapter 4
Information Handling

When you have finished this chapter, you should be able to describe

- [ ] the terms *data and information*
- [ ] the structure of information
- [ ] sources of information
- [ ] finding information
- [ ] sorting and searching for information
- [ ] types of information

4.1 Data and Information

At first, it may not seem that there is any difference between data and information. Quite often we use the words interchangeably. We might say "give us the data on road accidents in Britain last year" or we may say "give us the information on road accidents in Britain last year".   Each statement would be equally understood and would receive the same response.

However, in computing terms, there is a clear difference between the two terms, data and information. To explain this, consider the following example.

A child comes home from school and tells his parents that he got seven marks in his class test. This is a piece of data. The problem for the parents is that the number seven on its own does not tell how well their child has done in the test.

Activity 4.1

What else do the parents need to know for the child's mark to mean anything to them? Write your ideas in the box below.

Did your ideas include the maximum mark for the test, i.e. what the seven marks was out of, and what the pass mark was. If the child scored seven out of ten, i.e. achieved seventy per cent, and the pass mark was five, then the parents would be pleased. If the child scored seven out of a hundred, i.e. seven per cent, and the pass mark was fifty per cent, then the parents would probably be disappointed.

This illustrates an important process. In order that the child's mark can be understood by the parents, the data (seven marks) has to be compared with the maximum mark and the pass mark. In other words, in order that one piece of data becomes meaningful other data has to be available. The **data** has to be **processed**, i.e. in this case, calculations have to be made, to provide **information** for the parents.

4.2 The Structure of Information

In order to make information easy to understand and manage, it is necessary to structure information. The structure that is chosen for information depends on the type of information and for what it is to be used. In the following sections, we will look at different types of structure chosen for information. These are: an address, text in a letter, names and addresses, football scores.

A An Address

An Address of a person or a business has a structure to make it easy to use. If you were given the following address,

Easton
P D Jones
Woldington
12, Dean Street

you might find it difficult to understand. You will not know whether Woldington is part of Easton or the other way round. The address would be easier to follow if it were written:

P D Jones
12, Dean Street
Easton
Woldington

Each line of the address is a part of the place in the line below.

B Text in a Letter

Consider the layout of the letter below.

The Iron Trouser Company
Headway Towers, Inglethorpe, PP34 7GT

J M Brown
92, Raven's Way
Sondhurst
NG23 4FR

10th June 1999

Ref: Application for the Post of Programmer

Dear Mr Brown,

We would like to invite you to attend an interview for the above post at 2.00 pm on Wednesday the 24th June 1999.   Please would you confirm that this will be convenient.

Yours sincerely,

Mr F Moorcroft
Personnel Manager

You can see that it has a structure. Each piece of information is placed in a particular position to another. The address of the company is placed at the top, the address of the person to whom the letter is to be sent is placed below the company address, the date is placed below the address, the body of the letter is placed below this.   The name of the person sending the letter is placed at the bottom.

Most formal letters are structured in this way, although there can be some variation. Because of this structure, the reader of the letter can find the information required very easily. The reader can go straight to the bottom of the letter to see who has written it. If they have just found an old letter, the reader can look immediately to the date to see when it was written. The structure helps the reader.

C Names and Addresses in a Database

Databases are used to store large amounts of data which have to be structured so that the user can obtain the information in an easy-to-understand form.

An example is shown below.

EMPLOYEE NUMBER	EMPLOYEE NAME	ADDRESS	TELEPHONE NUMBER
1000012	Brown A J	10, The High Street, Loadley	714536
1000043	Davis V C	4, Litten Terrace, Loadley	725776
1000085	Fowey J D	23, The Lane, Cumbley	562431
1000098	Northey A	43, Main Street, Lotton	345932

Each row in the table of data above is called a **record** and each item in each row is called a **field**. The records are positioned in the table according to the employee number, so if the employee number is known then the name address and telephone number can be quickly found. This means that instead of storing the name and address of each employee in many different files, only the employee number needs to be stored.

D Numbers in Table

Consider the following table.

Team	Played	Won	Lost	Drawn	Points
The Badgers	3	3	0	0	6
Wondergirls	3	2	1	0	4
The Massive	3	0	2	1	1
Cool Ten	3	0	2	1	1

You can see that numbers are often best represented in the form of a table. A table has columns and rows. At the head of each column and the begining of each row is a heading. Each row is similar to a record in a database table.

The row with the heading The Badgers has five items of data in it showing the results of sports fixtures.

4.3 Sources of Information

Information can be found in many different places. We are surrounded by information. Wherever you can find information is called a **source**.

Activity 4.2

Think of the different places that you might find information and make a list of them in the box below.

Did your list include:

people
text books
atlases
dictionaries
magazines
advertisements
photographs
radio
television
compact discs
computers
the internet
packaging
timetables
lesson notes
coins and bank notes

The list seems to be endless. We spend much of our time taking in information from all around us. We chat to people, read numbers and words and look at diagrams and pictures. We are absorbing information from a wide range of information sources every moment of our waking day.

4.4 Finding Information

Although we live in an information age, information is no good to us unless we can find it in a suitable form. You need to be able to decide what information you want and then find it quickly.

Activity 4.3

Look at the list of sources of information above, think of the different methods used to find the information that you need and make a list of them in the box below.

Did your list include:

* for text books and atlases you would use **indexes** which are a list of contents sorted into alphabetical order with page numbers, placed at the back of a publication,
* dictionaries and telephone directories are **sorted** into alphabetical order,
* timetables are **sorted** into time order,
* television and radio programmes are **sorted** into time and day order,
* magazines and other publications have tables of **contents** at the front **sorted** into page number order,
* the internet uses **search machines** to find information,
* computer folders and files are **sorted** into alphabetical order within the folder structure,
* music on compact disc is **sorted** into track order, and
* information from computers or calculators may be produced when you **input or change values**, e.g. in a spreadsheet.

You can see from this that we find most of our information by having it sorted into alphabetic or numeric order.

4.5 Sorting and Searching for Information

Finding information requires that data be searched and for data to be searched effectively it needs to be sorted. Searching uses **rules or criteria** to find the data required. A search can be made using **relational operators** or a combination of relational operators and **logical operators**.

A Searching using Relational Operators

A file of data can be **searched** on a particular field or fields using **relational operators**. For example, for a car-share scheme, it would be necessary to group people according to location. The file can be searched by finding all those people who come from Hampshire.

The **criterion** would be the **condition**, | COUNTY = Hampshire.

The relational operator in this case is the equals symbol or =. Two other relational operators are

less than   <
greater than   >

These can be combined to give the additional relational operators

less than or equal to   <=
greater than or equal to   >=
not equal to   <>

Examples

If you wish to search for employees who worked for thirty hours or more in a particular week, the search criterion would be
   HOURS WORKED >= 30

If you wish to search for employees whose hourly rate is less than eight pounds per hour, the search criterion would be
   HOURLY RATE < 8.00

B Searching using Logical Operators

It is also possible to search a database using more complicated search criteria. Consider the following examples.

Example 1

Used cars can also be placed on a national database. If someone is looking for a Ford Escort for under £5,000 and which has travelled under 40,000 miles, the search criteria would be:

   MAKE=Ford AND
   TYPE=Escort AND
   PRICE<£5,000 AND
   MILEAGE<40,000

The cars fitting these criteria and their location would be printed in a report for the customer to consider.

In this example, **AND** is a **logical operator**.

Example 2

If someone is less fussy about his or her requirements for a car and wants either a Ford Escort or a Vauxhall Astra, the search criteria would be

> (MAKE=Ford **AND**
> TYPE=Escort) **OR**
> (MAKE=Vauxhall **AND**
> TYPE=Astra)

OR is another logical operator.

4.6 Types of Information

When information is stored in a computer, it is important to specify what type of information it is. This is part of the classification process. The data types used include:

Text or character. This means that the data is stored in the form of text characters. Names and Addresses are stored in this way. Numbers can be stored as text characters but, when this is done, calculations cannot be carried out with them.

Number. This is the data type used for numbers when they are to be used in any sort of calculation. This type has many different **formats** which include:

> **currency** for storing money values. For example, 1234 pounds would be stored as £1,234 or £1,234.00 if pence are to be shown.
>
> **decimal** for numbers with decimal part - called **real** numbers
>
> **integer** for whole numbers, i.e. numbers without decimal places.
>
> **percentage** such as 12.00%.

Date/time. This is the data type used for storing the date and the time. The date might be stored with the **format** 01/01/00 or 1st Jan 2000.

Formula. Sometimes a value might be stored as a formula. For example, the total in the Sales Figures spreadsheet shown earlier, would be a formula adding together the numbers in the column. If the numbers change, the value for the total will also change.

Function. This is a pre-determined formula that performs a calculation. An example is SUM which adds a set of values and AVE which calculates the average of a set of values.

Logical. This describes the values TRUE or FALSE.

Chapter 5
Handling Techniques

When you have finished this chapter, you should be able to describe

- hypertext databases
- record-structured databases
- number-structured databases

5.1 Databases

If you look up the definition of a database you will read something like the following:

A database is a collection of related data held in an organised way.

From a user's point of view, it is information held in a way that makes it easy to access.

Many of the sources of information listed in activity 1.2 are databases. A book catalogue in a bookshop or library, a list of films available in a video shop, a home shopping brochure and a list of staff telephone numbers at your place of work are all databases. If they are printed they are **paper-based** and if they are held on computer they are **computer-based**. In this book, when we use the term database, we mean a computer-based database.

We are going to consider three types of computer-based database:

hypertext databases, which are found on the **internet**,
record-structured databases, which are commonly known as **databases** and
number-structured databases, usually known as **spreadsheets**.

5.2 Hypertext Databases

A hypertext database is a number of pages of information made up of text and graphic images. It looks like a pages in a magazine. The internet has thousands of millions of pages like this available to its users. CD ROM encyclopaedias and other CD ROM-based data sources use this type of database.

An example of an internet page is shown on the next page.

Welcome To Liberty Hall's Home Page

Liberty Hall is an Educational Publishers who believe

books should be affordable and designed with the students in mind.

5.3 Record-Structured Databases

Record-structured databases are used to store large amounts of data so that the user can obtain the information he or she needs when required and in an easy-to-understand form. When the term *database* is used it geberally means *a record-structured database*.

These databases allow the user to select the information required and to ignore the rest. Different users can use different parts of the database but may not be allowed to obtain the information from other parts.

The most common type of database is called a **relational database**. In this type of database, the data is held in tables and each **table** has a number of rows.

The following example of a table was shown in section 4.2 C.

EMPLOYEE NUMBER	EMPLOYEE NAME	ADDRESS	TELEPHONE NUMBER
1000012	Brown A J	10, The High Street, Loadley	714536
1000043	Davis V C	4, Litten Terrace, Loadley	725776
1000085	Fowey J D	23, The Lane, Cumbley	562431
1000098	Northey A	43, Main Street, Lotton	345932

In most databases, there will be a number of tables, one for each type of item in the system. For example, there might be a table for customers, a table for suppliers, a table for products.

As well as the tables, the relationships between tables have to be defined. In other words, the relationship between products and suppliers and products and customers will be defined. This process links the tables together to form the complete database system. Hence the term **relational database.**

Record-structured information is used widely in the business and commercial world. Examples are:

Doctor's patient records will include patient number, name, address, telephone number, next of kin, health history.

Sales orders will include item number, description, quantity, price.

Stock records will include stock number, item, description, number in stock, supplier code, re-order level.

Bank records will include account number, name, address, type of account.

The software that manages the database is called a database management system. Access 2000 is a **relational database management system.**

Each row in the table above is called a **record**, in this case an employee record. Each item in the record is called a **field.**

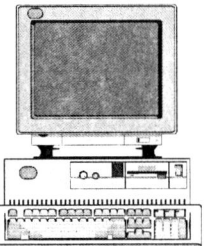

 Activity 5.1

1. Choose information that would be stored in a record-structured database.

2. Write down the fields that would make up a record in that database.

5.4 Number-Structured Databases

A number-structured database, called a spreadsheet, is like a large sheet of paper, ruled in columns and rows, and a calculator: but rather than being on paper, it is displayed on a computer screen with all the information held in the computer. It allows the user to store data, names and numbers and do calculations. A simple spreadsheet might be:

Salesperson	Sales		
	Oct	Nov	Dec
Brown, A	£2,300	£3,100	£1,900
Green, B	£3,500	£4,200	£3,600
Gray, J	£1,600	£2,000	£2,100
TOTAL	£7,400	£9,300	£7,600

You can see that the spreadsheet has names numbers and calculated totals.

In order to insert data the spreadsheet is divided into cells and each cell has a unique reference.   A picture of the Excel spreadsheet is shown below:

	A	B	C	D
1				
2				
3				
4				
5				
6				
7				

Each column has a unique letter and each row a number.   Each cell, therefore, has a **cell reference**. The highlighted cell above is cell C6.

Spreadsheets can be used to carry out calculations as in the totals shown above and produce graphs and charts such as that shown below.

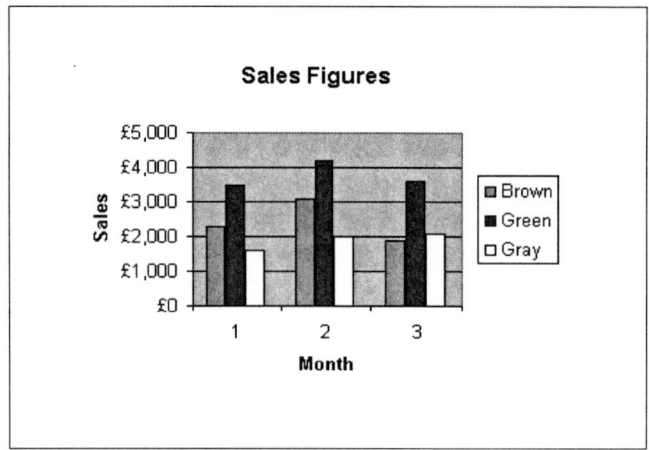

Number-structured information is used widely in the business and commercial world, usually for financial and accounting activities. Examples are:

Sales forecasting
Balance sheet
Mortgage and interest calculations.

They are also used in mathematical and scientific applications, e.g.

Weather forecasting
Statistical calculations
Materials testing.

Chapter 6
Design of Information Handling Systems

When you have finished this chapter, you should be able to

- prepare the design
- implement the solution

6.1 Preparing the Design

Information handling systems based on spreadsheets or databases can be described by the following diagram.

Data and information are input to the system.   This is processed to produce output.

To design a data handling system, therefore, you have to consider these three stages.

A   Output Requirements

The data handling system you are to design will exist to produce something, i.e. to produce output.   The starting point, therefore, is to consider the output requirements.

For example, if you are designing a system to produce membership details for a club and the output is to be displayed on screen and in printed form, you will need to produce examples of screen layouts, printer output and templates.   These should be drawn on paper.

The ouput can be in the form of:

Printed text   Information handling systems often produce text output

Charts and Graphs   Some information is often better displayed in the form of graphs or charts. These include:

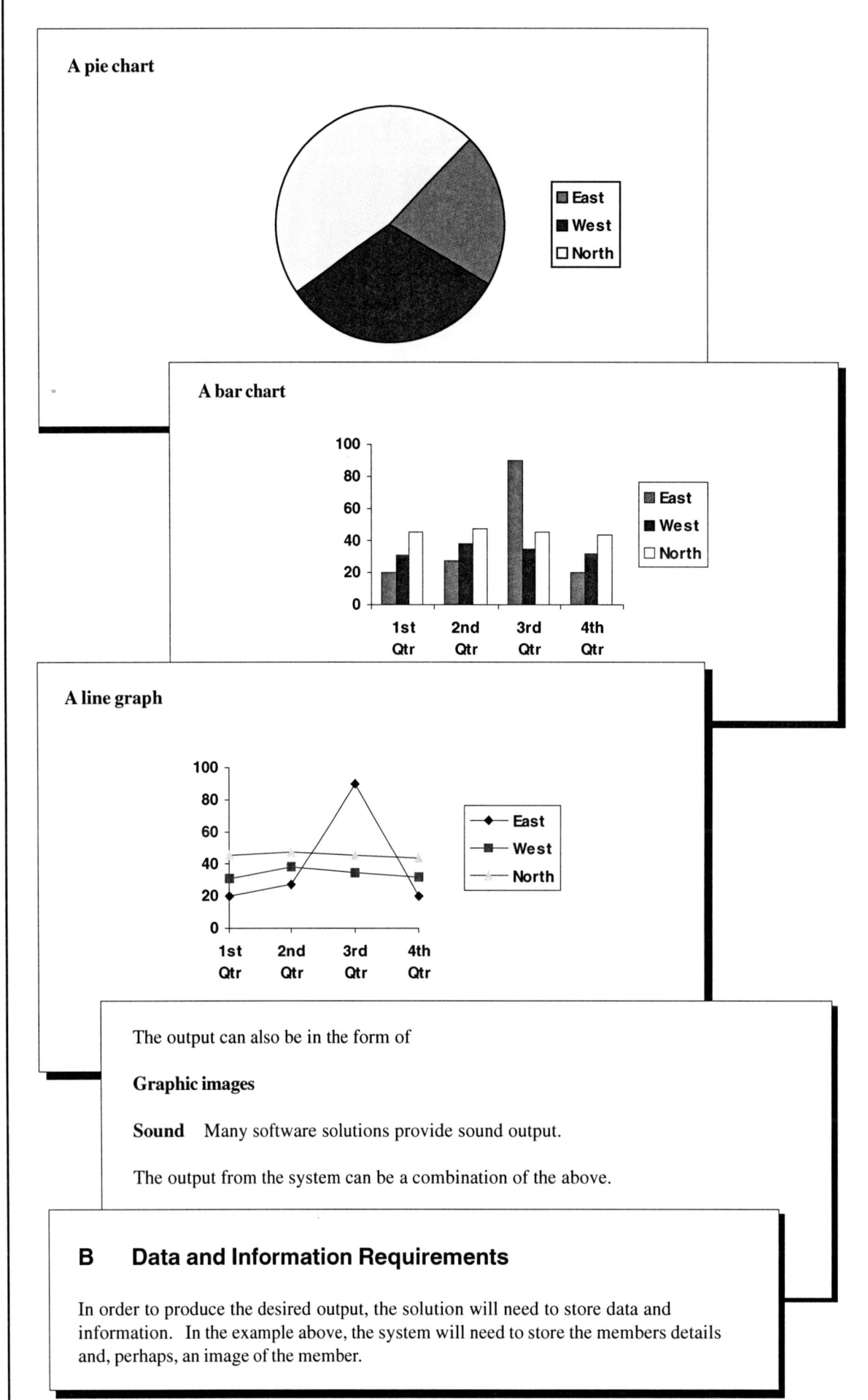

A pie chart

A bar chart

A line graph

The output can also be in the form of

Graphic images

Sound Many software solutions provide sound output.

The output from the system can be a combination of the above.

B Data and Information Requirements

In order to produce the desired output, the solution will need to store data and information. In the example above, the system will need to store the members details and, perhaps, an image of the member.

C Input Requirements

When the data storage requirements are known, the input requirments can be determined. In the example above, the input requirements are member details and a scanned image of the member.

D Processing Requirements

You now have to consider the processes that need to take place to produce the required output from the input data and the stored information. There are a wide range of processing activities, which include:

Calculations Many processes include calculations. Input data and stored data will be included in these to produce values to be included in the output. Making calculations will involve using formulae.

Formulae Formulae is a set of instructions which represent a calculation. Formulae include data values and functions.

Functions These are a pre-determined set of calculations. A calculation can involve functions.

What if processing or hypothesis testing This is the process of entering different input data to examine the effect on the output. You answer the question *what happens to the output if the input values are altered?*

Sorting This is the process of organising data into a sequence. It can be alphabetic for text and numeric for numbers. Information can be sorted into **ascending** order, i.e. from the lowest value to the highest, or **descending**, from the highest to the lowest.

Searching This is the process of looking for particular items of data. Searching involves the use of search criteria which use **relational operators** such as =, <, >, <>, <= and >= and **logical operators** such as AND, OR and NOT. Very complex searches can be created using a combination of these operators.

Selecting This is the process of extracting data from a data store following a search.

E Software Requirements

You now have to confirm the software that will best achieve the needs of the users. The software chosen will have to be able to:

produce output in the desired format
store data in a suitable format
accept data in an acceptable way.

You will have to decide whether a database or spreadsheet software is the most suitable for a solution. For processing involving many calculations and requiring chart or graph output, a spreadsheet is likely to provide the best facilities. For processing that requires sorting, searching and selecting a database solution is most likely the best.

If you are working with the Internet, you will have to choose software that will make it possible to write the web pages and allow orders to be placed with the client.

If templates are to be created or macros written, you will have to be sure that the software has the correct facilities. If you need good graphics, you will have to be sure that the software supports it.

6.2 Implementing the Design

When your design has been planned, you can get down to implementing the design. This will include:

defining the needs of the users. Computer-based systems are produced for users. The user or client might be a company, a small organisation, such as a club or an invidual. If you are writing a system for yourself, then you are the user. Careful thought and analysis has to be carried out so that the needs of the users are determined.

This will lead to:

defining the purpose of the system. A clear statement of the purpose of the system has to be produced. Without this the work of producing the system will be very difficult and maybe impossible.

defining the output needs. As stated in the last section, this is the first stage to consider. You have to determine what the user wants from the system. Even though it might seem logical, you should not start with the input requirements: they canot be determined without knowing the desired outputs.

defining the data and information storage requirements. The next stage is to look at the way that information and data will be stored and organised in the system.

defining the input needs. You can now determine the data and information that will need to be input to create the desired outputs.

defining the processing needs. Some of the data will need to be processed to produce the desired output. These need to be determined before the system is created.

choosing the software and creating the storage structures. The software to be used should be chosen. The software will need to be able to create the storage structures required, carry out the necessary processing and produce the required output.

collecting the data and information for storage Where necessary, you will need to design methods for collecting the data that will be input to the system.

entering the data and information Once the system is written, data and information can be entered. At first this will be test data. When the system is working according to the specification, the real data can be entered. This will allow you to:

process the data and information and

produce the required output information.

Chapter 7
Database Methods

When you have finished this chapter, you should be able to descibe

- database terms
- database design
- constructing a database

7.1 Database Terms

When we use the term database, we mean record-structured database. In chapter 2, a **relational database** was described using the following example.

EMPLOYEE NUMBER	EMPLOYEE NAME	ADDRESS	TELEPHONE NUMBER
1000012	Brown A J	10, The High Street, Loadley	714536
1000043	Davis V C	4, Litten Terrace, Loadley	725776
1000085	Fowey J D	23, The Lane, Cumbley	562431
1000098	Northey A	43, Main Street, Lotton	345932

This is a database **table** containing data about employees.

A   Record

Each row in the table is called a **record**. The record for A J Brown is, therefore,

| 1000012 | Brown A J | 10, The High Street, Loadley | 714536 |

B   Field

This record has a number of **fields**:

1000012	is a field,
Brown A J	is a field,
10, The High Street, Loadley	is a field, and
714536	is a field.

Each of these fields tells you something about A J Brown - his name, address and phone number.

C   Primary Key

The first field is a special field called the **primary key** field. This has a special job - it makes the record **unique**. This means that no two records can be the same.

You may not at first think that this field is necessary, but it is possible for two people to live in the same house with the same names and to work at the same company, for instance, a father and son. In this case, each of these would have a different employee number, i.e. a different value in the primary key field.

The primary key field is used to extract details from the database. You can ask for details of the employee with the number 1000043 and will only get the details of one person. If you tried to use any other field for this type of search, you might get more than one employee's details being extracted, creating confusion, e.g. two people could have the same name, or the same phone number and address.

Primary keys are used in many different databases. In a payroll database, each employee would be given a payroll number. In a stock control system each item of stock would be given a stock number. In a video shop, each video would be given a video number.

D   Foreign Key

In a relational database, there will be a number of tables of data, one for each entity in the system. An entity is an item such as EMPLOYEE in the table above. Each table of data will have records and a primary key field.

If a field in one table, not the primary key field, is the primary key field in another table in the same database, it is said to be the **foreign key** in the table where it is not the primary key.

E   Field Name and Length

Each field in a record is given a **field name**. The field names in the example above are

EMPLOYEE NUMBER, EMPLOYEE NAME, ADDRESS and TELEPHONE NUMBER.

Each of these fields will have a **field length**. This is the size of the field. For a name the field length might be 30 characters, i.e. you will be able to key in up to 30 letters for a name. For an address field, 100 characters will be allowed. This will contain letters and numbers.

A field that holds a number, which may be used in a calculation, will have a size that allows all the digits of a number to be stored. The larger the number, the larger the field size needed.

F   Field Data Types

Each field has a data type. This tells you what type of data is to be held in the field. The types include:

text, for storing alphabetic and numeric characters, e.g. UB40,
number, for storing numbers, e.g. 123, -345.67 and 0.45637,
currency, for storing money values, e.g. £1,200 and £29.45, and
date, for storing dates such as 01/02/2000.

7.2 Database Design

It is important to know that, in order to develop good database systems, design is important. In large collections of data there is the possibility for the same data to be stored a number of times. This is called **data duplication**. Some duplication is necessary but computerised database systems are constructed to reduce the amount of duplication.

To understand why duplication is a problem we will consider the storage of names and addresses in a large company computer. Staff names and addresses will be needed for different purposes and may be stored on separate files.

The problem with having separate files is that as staff move home, not all the files will be altered appropriately. Because the data is duplicated it is difficult to keep accurately up-to-date. The payroll file might be updated but the pensions file may not. When this happens the **integrity** of the data is lost., i.e. you cannot believe the data in the system. **Data duplication leads to a loss of data integrity.**

In a computerised database system the names and addresses of the staff would be held only once and these would be used for payroll, personnel, pensions and social club activities.

Before a database system can be produced, it is necessary to produce a database specification. A process called systems analysis is used to create the database specification.

The design and creation of a database has a number of steps. These are described below.

A   User Needs

The database specification will include a description of the purpose of the database and the needs of the user, i.e. you need to know what the user requires from the database system and what the system is for.

B   Information Needs

One of the most important stages in the design of a database system, is to determine what information is to be produced by it. The database specification will include, therefore, a description of the output information required. This is called the **output specification**.

When the output required has been determined, it is necessary to decide the information that has to be stored in the database, i.e. an **input specification** is required.

7.3 Case Study - North Barchester College

In this example, we will use a case study concerned with the learning activities in North Barchester College. This college serves a medium-sized town surrounded by farmland. It has 1000 full-time students and 2,000 part-time students. It runs full-year courses and short courses. All its students are over 15 years of age. All students have to enrol on their courses.

An enrolment involves one student and one course. A student can make a number of enrolments, but each enrolment involves only one student and one course. A course can have many enrolments.

This can be represented by the following diagram.

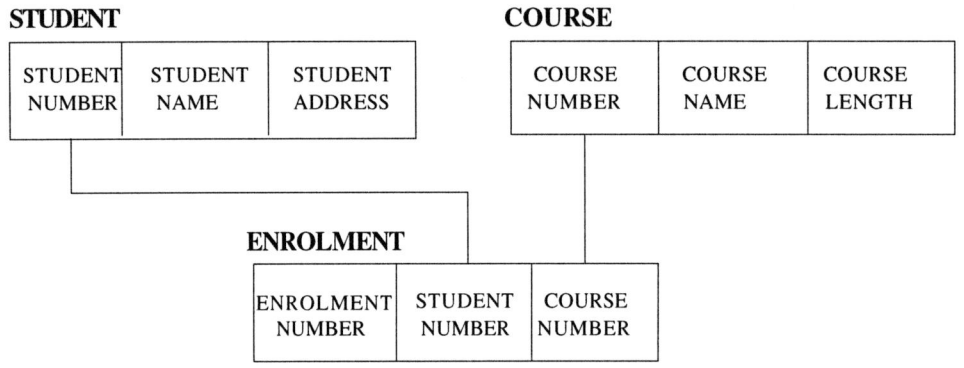

This is a model of the enrolment system. STUDENT NUMBER is the key field in the **STUDENT** record and a foreign key in the **ENROLMENT** record. COURSE NUMBER is the key field in the **COURSE** record and a foreign key in the **ENROLMENT** record.

The ENROLMENT record is created so that each time a student enrols on a course there is no need to key in the student's name and address.

7.4 Constructing a Database

In this unit, you are expected to construct a simple database.

A database is created using special software. An example is Microsoft Access 2000, which is a **relational database management system**, i.e. it is computer software that allows you to create a database, enter and alter data in the database, search and sort data in the database and produce the required output.

This type of software is easy-to-use and users with little programming experience can produce very powerful database systems.

Database software allows you to create tables with records and fields, specify data types, enter and alter data and design and produce output.

For the North Barchester College case study described above you would need to carry out the following steps.

A   Create the Tables

The first stage is to create three tables for STUDENT, COURSE and ENROLMENT. In Microsoft Access, you would create these using the Tables button and clicking on Create Table in design view. This will allow you to set up the record with its fields, set the field length, field types and the primary key.

B   Set the Relationships

The second stage is to set the relationships between the tables. This will link the STUDENT table to the ENROLMENT table by tying the primery key to the foreign key as in the diagram above, and the COURSE table to the ENROLMENT table.

C   Enter the Data

It is very important that data that is stored in a database is correct. Data has to be collected before it can be entered. Data collection is usually carried out using forms. People fill forms in and the data from them is keyed into the database system. Sometimes the form will be on a computer screen but often it will be on paper.

The data entered will be checked for errors first by people, probably by the person entering the data, and then by the computer.

The data entered will be converted into database records which will be stored in its logical place in the system. This will involve sorting the data.

D   Searching the Database

A database is created so that users can get information from it. In order to do so, the database has to be searched.

Search criteria have to be set up before the data can be searched. These are the rules that will apply to the search. For example, you may be searching a housing database for a flat in your area with a price you can afford.

The computer might ask you the following questions (the answers are in italics):

Which area are you interested in? *Malling*

What type of dwelling? *Flat*

What price range? *£50, 000 to £70,000*

The user will use the following search criteria to retrieve the information required. *See chapter 3, section 3.3 for a description of searching.*

AREA = Malling **AND**
TYPE = Flat **AND**
PRICE >= 50000 **AND**
PRICE <= 70000

All the records in the database that satisfy the search criteria will be made available to the user. Before the data is presented to the user, it may need to be sorted.

Searching and Sorting are implemented using the Queries facilty in Microsoft Access.

E   Producing the Output

The output produced from a database is called a **report**. This can be output produced on a printer or on the computer screen.

Database software has special facilities to make producing reports easy. One common facility is the **report wizard**. This has a set of styles of report from which you can choose. If you want more complicated reports, programmers can write additional software to produce this. Most users will be able to produce all the reports they need using the wizard.

In Microsoft Access, the **Reports** button will be used.

    Activity 7.1

In this activity, the tables for a North Barchester College database will be produced for each of the following entities:

Student
Course
Enrolment

1.   Create a new database with the title COLLEGE.

   *Click on **File** in the Menu bar, select **New**, click the **Database** icon under the **General** tab, click **OK**, select drive A, type **COLLEGE** and click on **Create**.*

2.   Create a new Table.   *Click on **Create table in Design view**.*

3.   Create the following Fields.

Field Name	Data Type	Description	Format
STUDNO	Number	Student identifying number	Long Integer
STUDNAME	Text	Name of student	50 characters
ADDRESS1	Text	First line of student's address	50 characters
ADDRESS2	Text	Second line of student's address	50 characters
ADDRESS3	Text	Third line of student's address	50 characters
POSTCODE	Text	Post code of student's address	10 characters
TELNO	Text	Student's phone number	20 characters

4.   Select STUDNO as the primary key.

5.   Save the Table design by closing the Design window.   Save it with the name STUDENT.

6.   Open the Table for data entry.   *Click on the **Open** button.*

7.   Enter the following data into the Table.
   You will need to alter the column widths to accommodate the data on the screen.

Activity 4.1 (continued)

STUDNO	STUDNAME	ADDRESS1	ADDRESS2	ADDRESS3	POSTCODE	TELNO
100001	Brown J	10 Monk Street	Newdigan	Cheshire	QA1 4DG	01995-637854
100002	Manser P	19 Knowle Way	South Digan	Cheshire	QA2 7YH	01995-694321
100003	Brewer S	4 High Street	Newdigan	Cheshire	QA1 7GH	01995-638920
100004	Smith K L	The Rectory	Church Lane	Mickleham	QB7 9AS	01903-567398
100005	Myers P N	10 The Byeways	Mickleham	Cheshire	QB9 6DF	01903-563927
100006	Tyson J J	Waterways	The Knowle	South Digan	QA2 9GB	01995-694471
100007	Delors J	22 Malt Way	Bigginton	Cheshire	QA4 5MN	01995-776530
100008	Able T	19 Watergate	Newdigan	Cheshire	QA1 8FG	01995-638710
100009	Chivers Y	99 Eastgate	Malmesford	Lancashire	QT9 4WM	01879-447733
100010	Peeble J	4 May Road	South Digan	Cheshire	QA2 4DL	01995-694822
100011	McCabe X	42 Galt Street	North Digan	Cheshire	QA4 6TF	01995-453678
100012	Evregard N	12 Main Road	Mickleham	Cheshire	QB1 2AS	01903-562987
100013	Fredricks L	32 Bell Lane	Newdigan	Cheshire	QA1 3WB	01995-638172
100014	Williams W	12a The Court	Bigginton	Cheshire	QA4 9PP	01995-779843
100015	Udall Q	62 Myrtle Road	Malmesford	Lancashire	QT8 3CV	01879-441212
100016	Norton K	1 Cavendish Street	South Digan	Cheshire	QA2 0LN	01995-694432
100017	Brent S	32 Browning Avenu	Mickleham	Cheshire	QB5 8CM	01903-562288
100018	Gillies P	8 Highfield Road	Newdigan	Cheshire	QA1 6TT	01995-638720
100019	Neeson A	84 Windermere Ro	Newdigan	Cheshire	QA1 1AL	01995-631111
100020	Gulliver T	72 Honeycrock Lar	Bigginton	Cheshire	QA4 7TY	01995-778340

8. Save the data.

9. Create a new Table.

10. Create the following Fields:

Field Name	Data Type	Description	Format
COURSENO	Number	Course identifying number	Long Integer
COURSENAME	Text	Name of course	50 characters
EXAMBODY	Text	Name of the examination body	50 characters
LEVEL	Text	Academic level of the course	50 characters

11. Select COURSENO as the primary key.

12. Save the Table design by closing the Design window. Save it with the name COURSE.

13. Open the Table for data entry.

14. Enter the following data into the Table.

COURSENO	COURSENAME	EXAMBODY	LEVEL
200001	Psychology	AEB	A
200002	Physics	AEB	A
200003	Mathematics	Oxford	A
200004	English	Cambridge	A
200005	Information Technology - GNVQ	BTEC	Intermediate
200006	Information Technology - GNVQ	BTEC	Advanced
200007	Media: Communication and Production - GNVQ	BTEC	Intermediate
200008	Media: Communication and Production - GNVQ	BTEC	Advanced
200009	English	SEG	GCSE
200010	Mathematics	SEG	GCSE
200011	Word Processing	RSA	1
200012	Word Processing	RSA	2

Activity 4.1 (continued)

15. Save the data.

16. Create a new Table.

17. Create the following Fields:

Field Name	Data Type	Description	Format
STUDNO	Number	Student identifying number	Long Integer
COURSENO	Number	Course identifying number	Long Integer

18. Save the Table design by closing the Design window.   Save it with the name ENROLMENT.

19. Open the Table for data entry.

20. Enter the following data into the Table.

STUDNO	COURSENO
100007	200001
100007	200003
100016	200005
100019	200005
100002	200006
100001	200004
100001	200003
100001	200002

21. Set the relationships between the tables according to the diagram in section 7.3.

22. Print out each table in the form of a report.

23. Use a query to produce a table of the students names and telephone numbers for the students on each course.

24. Print this table.

Chapter 8
Spreadsheet Methods

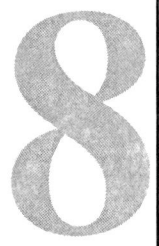

When you have finished this chapter, you should be able to describe

- spreadsheet terms
- what-if testing
- creating charts and graphs

8.1 Spreadsheet Terms

Spreadsheets are number-structured databases. From this you can tell that this type of database is designed to store mainly numbers, although it also stores text and formulae. A formula is a set of actions that form a calculation.

In chapter 5, a spreadsheet was described as being similar to a large sheet of paper, ruled in columns and rows and a calculator.

Example

A set of students score the following marks in three tests.

Student	Marks			
	Test 1	Test 2	Test 3	Average
Davidson, D	78	65	80	
Baker, G	45	50	37	
Willaims, N	90	84	75	

This information will be keyed into a spreadsheet to produce:

	A	B	C	D	E	F	G
1							
2							
3	Student			Marks			
4							
5			Test 1	Test 2	Test 3	Average	
6							
7	Davidson, D		78	65	80		
8	Baker, G		45	50	37		
9	Williams, N		90	84	75		
10							
11							
12							

A Cells and Cell References

You can see from the spreadsheet, that each item of information is stored in a different box. Each box is called a **cell**. Each cell can be referred to by its column letter and its row number, e.g. the word *Student* is in cell A3, and the number 80 is in cell E7. A3 and E7 are called **cell references**.

B Formulae

The averages have to be calculated using a **formula**. For the first student, D Davidson, the average needs to be stored in cell F7. The formula used could be

value in F7 = **(C7+D7+E7)/3**

This is telling the software to add the contents of C7, D7 and E7, divide this total by three and place the result into F7. To do this, the part of the formula in bold is keyed into the cell F7.

C Relative and Absolute Cell References

The cell references in the formula above, C7, D7, and E7 are **relative cell references** because they relate to the cell F7, the cell that contains the formula. If this formula was copied to F8, the value placed in F8 would be the result **(C8+D8+E8)/3** not **(C7+D7+E7)/3**. In our example, this would be the average for G Baker.

An **absolute cell reference** always refers to a particular cell in the spreadsheet. You can place a value in this cell and use it in calculations in different areas of the spreadsheet.

Microsoft Excel uses the $ sign to distinguish absolute cell references from relative cell references, e.g. A7 is the absolute cell reference for cell A7.

D Functions

You can see from this, that if you were averaging the results from twenty tests, the formula would be very long and would be difficult and time-consuming to key in. In order to simplify matters, the formula can use a **function**, in this case the function AVERAGE.

Using AVERAGE, the formula will become

value in F7 = **AVERAGE(C7:E7)**

The individual cell references have been replaced by the **range**, C7:E7, to make it easier to type.

There are many different mathematical functions available, including **SUM** which is used to make totals of numbers.

With the formulae added to the spreadsheet it will become

	A	B	C	D	E	F	G
1							
2							
3	Student			Marks			
4							
5			Test 1	Test 2	Test 3	Average	
6							
7	Davidson, D		78	65	80	74.33333	
8	Baker, G		45	50	37	44	
9	Williams, N		90	84	75	83	
10							

E   Cell Format

You can see now that there is a new problem. One of the averages has a lot of decimal places and the presentation does not look as tidy as it might.

To change this the **format** of the cells containing numbers has to be altered. The numbers need to have no decimal places, they need to be **integer** numbers. This adjustment can be made to the spreadsheet to produce:

	A	B	C	D	E	F	G
1							
2							
3	Student			Marks			
4							
5			Test 1	Test 2	Test 3	Average	
6							
7	Davidson, D		78	65	80	74	
8	Baker, G		45	50	37	44	
9	Williams, N		90	84	75	83	
10							

F   IF .. THEN .. ELSE

It is possible to apply an IF function to a cell which will return a TRUE or FALSE. For example, if you stored the examination results of a set of students in a spreadsheet as follows:

STUDENT	MARK	RESULT
Able, A	32	
Baker, B	76	
Cook, C	55	

you may wish to enter the words PASS or FAIL in the RESULT column if the students mark was 50 or over.

To do this you would use the function

IF (MARK>49 **THEN** PASS **ELSE** FAIL).

This will produce the following:

STUDENT	MARK	RESULT
Able, A	32	FAIL
Baker, B	76	PASS
Cook, C	55	PASS

The expression MARK>49 is called the logical test and the symbol > is called the relational operator. The relational operators are:

=	equals
>	greater than
<	less than
<>	not equal to
<=	less than or equal to
>=	greater than or equal to

8.2 What-if Testing

It is possible to use a spreadsheet to test different ideas. You can change the input to see what happens to the output.

For instance, a spreadsheet might be used to predict the temperature in different rooms in a house when the outside temperature is changing and different activities are taking place in the house, e.g. cooking and bathing.

When the spreadsheet has been set up, values can be altered to see the effects on temperature. This is called **what-if** testing, e.g. **what** happens to the room temperature **if** the outside temperature falls to 0 degrees Centigrade and someone is taking a bath.

The spreadsheet set up for this purpose is called a numerical **model**.

This method can be use for forecasting. An example would be predicting future profits of a business. A spreadsheet numerical model of the business's activities would be created. Different values can then be altered to see the effect on profit. For example, the cost of materials and the selling price could be altered to see what happens to the profit.

8.3 Case Study - ComCom Inc

ComComInc produces computer components. One of ComCom Inc's first products is a PC tower chassis. The company intend to commence their production in the first quarter of the next financial year. The market for these tower units is a range of PC manufacturers who are assembling their own name PC's.

A small factory unit has been leased and equipped with all the necessary tools and machinery.

The details are as follows:

Cost: £64,000

The manager in charge of production has costed out the manufacturing, based on all the necessary materials and labour associated with building the units.

Initial Cost: £24.60 per unit

The manager in charge of business development is determined that they should sell their product at a competitive price.

Initial Price: £38.00 per unit

Setting up the company is a complex business and they need to do some detailed calculations before they start selling the units. In order to be able to plan their business effectively, the partners wish to know how many units they have to make and sell before they cover all costs and start to make a profit. This is going to be crucial if they are to convince the bank manager to provide them with a business start-up loan.

This problem is a typical business problem, involving numbers, that can be **modelled** using a computer. In order to provide a solution for the partners, we will set up details of the costs and income on a spreadsheet model. Our model is not a physical model like a plastic 1/32 scale kit, but a **numerical model** that allows us to pretend or **simulate** the real operating conditions.

At this stage we don't know how many tower units we need to make before we start making a profit. What we do know is if we don't make enough units the costs will be greater than the income. After selling a certain quantity the income will be greater than the costs and we will make a profit. At one point the costs will be equal to the income, making no profit and no loss; this point is the **break even point**. This is the information we are going to provide to the partners. By setting our solution up as a computer model we can try altering many of the **variables** such as the cost per unit, or selling price per unit and see what effect this will have. This is **what if** modelling.

The Solution

We are going to look at the costs, income and profit based on a number of possible quantities that may be sold, ranging from 0 to 8000 in steps of 1000.

Let's represent the number of tower units that may be sold by the letter T

Fixed cost   =   64000   [1]

Stays at £64000 regardless of the number of towers made

Variable cost =   24.60T   [2]

Varies according to the number of towers made, at £24.60 per tower

Total cost   =   24.60T + 64000   [3]

Sum of both costs

> *24.60T is*
>
> *24.60 times T*

The Solution (continued)

Income = 38.00T   [4]

Varies according to the number of towers sold, at £38 per tower

Profit = Income - Costs   [4] - [3]

Now to build up our model......

The following spreadsheet represents the model.

Quantity	0	1000	2000	3000	4000	5000	6000	7000	8000
Total Cost	64000	86000	113200	137800	162400	187000	211600	236200	260800
Income	0	38000	76000	114000	152000	190000	228000	266000	304000
Profit	-64000	-50600	-37200	-23800	-10400	3000	16400	29800	43200

We can now see that somewhere between sales of 4000 and 5000 tower units they will 'break even'. Our model so far does not allow us to be any more accurate. There are a number of ways we could find the precise figure.

We could do this by:

A   producing a graph of the data and reading the value off the graph, or

B   carrying out a calculation based on Costs = Income at the break even point, or

C   using 'goal-seeking' techniques on a spreadsheet.

A   Graphing

A graph can be produced from the spreadsheet to show the value as follows:

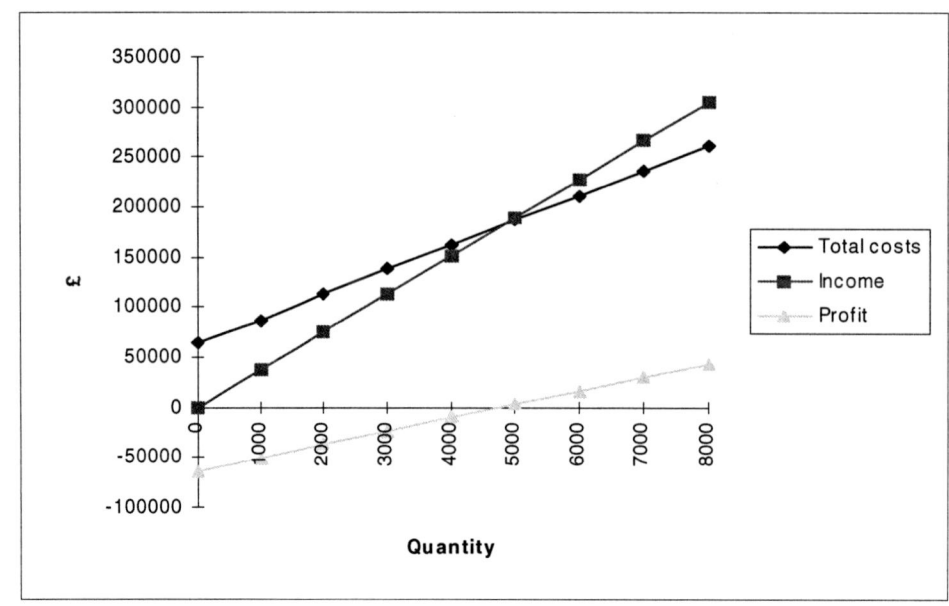

B   Calculation

At the break even point   Costs = Income

so   24.6T + 64000 = 38T

so   13.4T = 64000 (£13.40 is the profit made per tower unit)

so   T = 64000/13.4

so   T = 4776 (zero decimal places)

C   Using Goal Seeking Techniques

Using the table of values that you set up to produce the graph, use **goal seek** in your spreadsheet package by setting the profit to zero by altering the quantity cell.

D   What-if Techniques

If you had set up your spreadsheet 'model' so that each variable was based in an independent 'absolute' cell, you could ask - what if the fixed cost goes up to £70000? This sort of computer based model makes it very easy to get the solution to these sort of questions.

Activity 8.1

Set up your own spreadsheet model based on the information provided in the case study. Create the break even graph and clearly mark the break even point and break even quantity.

Note: make the fixed and variable costs, and the selling price 'absolute cells'.

Having set up your model can you answer these questions?

1   How many tower units should ComCom sell in order to break even?

2   How much should they charge in order to break even if they have to sell a minimum of 3500 units?

3   'What if' the company decides that it wishes to increase the selling price by 20% to compensate for an increase in all the costs of 12%

   (i)   What is the new selling price?
   (ii)   What will the new costs be?
   (iii) What is the new break even quantity?

4   Using your computer 'model' demonstrate how you would establish the number of units that should be sold at the new price if the company expects to make a £20000 profit.

8.4 Producing Charts and Line Graphs

As you can see in the case study above, one popular way of presenting output from a computer is to produce a visual representation of information in the form of a chart or graph.

Spreadsheet software has special facilities to make producing reports easy. One common facility is the wizard. This has a set of types of chart from which you can choose.

In this unit, you will need to be able to create charts and graphs with clear titles and labels, including:

Main titles
Axis titles
Axis scale labels
Legend titles
Data or series labels

You will also need to be able to select colours and patterns for the charts.

 **Now It's Time to Test Yourself!**

Multiple choice

1. Which of the following is **not** an information source?

   a. newspaper
   c. underlining
   b. timetable
   d. radio

2. In a text book, you can find information using:

   a. a chapter
   c. sorting
   b. the cover
   d. an index

3. Which of the following is a relational operator?

   a. AND
   c. OR
   b. <>
   d. equals

4. Which of the following is a logical operator?

   a. AND
   c. =
   b. <>
   d. <

5. Which of the following is **not** a data type?

   a. formula
   c. operator
   b. number
   d. text

6. Which of the following is a spreadsheet term?

   a. cell
   c. field
   b. record
   d. primary key

7. Hypertext pages are used:

   a. on the internet
   c. in text documents
   b. in spreadsheets
   d. in record-structured databases

8. A relational database is:

   a. a number-structured database
   c. a record-structured database
   b. a hypertext database
   d. paper-based database

9. Which of the following is **not** a processing activity?

   a. programming
   c. searching
   b. sorting
   d. calculating

10. Which of the following is a database term?

    a. cell
    c. formula
    b. record
    d. cell reference

Assessment
Unit 2

In this unit, you are to create a database with at least two tables and a spreadsheet.

You must produce the following **Assessment Evidence**:

1. a relational database and a spreadsheet to meet user needs. These must include a description of the system and annotated printed output demonstrating its operation and showing how it meets user needs.

2. an evaluation of your work.

The criteria only need to be met once for this unit. Except where stated otherwise, they may be met in either your database or your spreadsheet.

If you are successful, you will be awarded a Pass, Merit or a Distinction according to the following.

Pass

To achieve a Pass your work must show:

P1 a clear description of the user's needs, the information to be processed and the processing required.

P2 table structures created using suitable field names, field lengths, data types, primary keys and relations.

P3 suitable spreadsheet created using row heights, column widths, cell formats, titles, cell references, IF ... THEN statements, arithmetic functions and formulae.

P4 your ability to use data-processing skills to enter data, sort, search, calculate, predict results, produce different types of charts or line graphs and create printed reports using related tables.

P5 you have produced printed copy showing that you have met the above require ments and explaining your work. This may include screen prints or annotated data output.

P6 your ability to check the accuracy of your data and keep backup copies of all files.

Merit

To achieve a Merit your work must **also** show:

M1 effective use of software to sort on multiple fields, make use of cell relationships and produce good quality printed copy, showing both data content, formats and formulae. Clear and detailed annotation, screen prints or notes must explain why and how all printed items are produced.

M2 a good use of titles, graphic lines, spacing, text size, text enhancement, column and row headers, page headers or footers and graph labels to enhance the presentations, making them easy to read and free of layout errors.

M3 you have checked your work for accuracy and corrected obvious errors.

M4 your ability to work independently to produce your work to agreed deadlines by carrying out your work plans effectively.

M5 clear progression from the design stage to completion and evaluation.

Distinction

To achieve a Distinction your work must **also** show:

D1 an in-depth understanding of database and spreadsheet systems and evaluate your work to make suggestions for improvement and to describe any problems experienced.

D2 use technical language fluently and produce clear, coherent and comprehensive explanations and annotations.

D3 make effective and efficient use of complex search criteria on related tables, formulae and absolute cell references to produce the desired outcomes.

Unit 3   Hardware and Software
by John Ayres

This unit is called **Hardware and Software**.

It will help you to:

- understand **ICT specifications** for hardware and software
- **select an ICT system** and **configure** it to meet the needs of users
- **write a program** to improve **efficient use** of application software
- write a program to display **hypertext information**
- understand and develop **good practice** and **standard ways of working** with ICT

You will configure operating system software and applications software to meet user needs and write some short programs.

What you have learned in Unit 1: *Presenting information* and Unit 2: *Handling Information* will help you in this unit.

This unit is assessed through your portfolio work only.   The grade for that assessment will be your grade for the unit.

Chapter 9
Hardware

Objectives

At the end of this chapter you will be able to describe

- an ICT system
- input devices
- output devices
- the central processing unit (cpu)
- auxiliary storage

9.1 An ICT System

An Information and Communication Technology (ICT) system consists of items of **hardware**, **software** and a human user to issue instructions.

The hardware elements are the items of equipment that are connected together to enable the processes to be carried out. Computer processes convert the input data into the output data in accordance with the instructions included in a program.

Software
This is all the programs that are stored in the computer system that enable the computer to carry out its tasks. It includes the programs that are needed to make the system run, such as the operating system and the applications, such as Word.

Hardware
This is all the machines and physical components of a computer system. It includes the system box containing the mother board, the central processing unit, the memory, various cards and the disc drives. It also includes input devices such as keyboard and mouse and output devices such as laser printer and visual display unit.

This is illustrated by the following diagram:

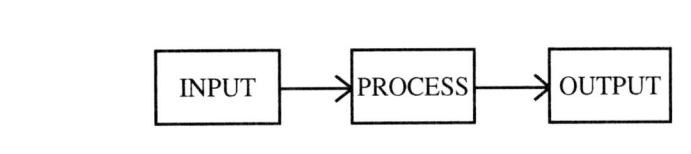

A typical configuration of such a system would be :-

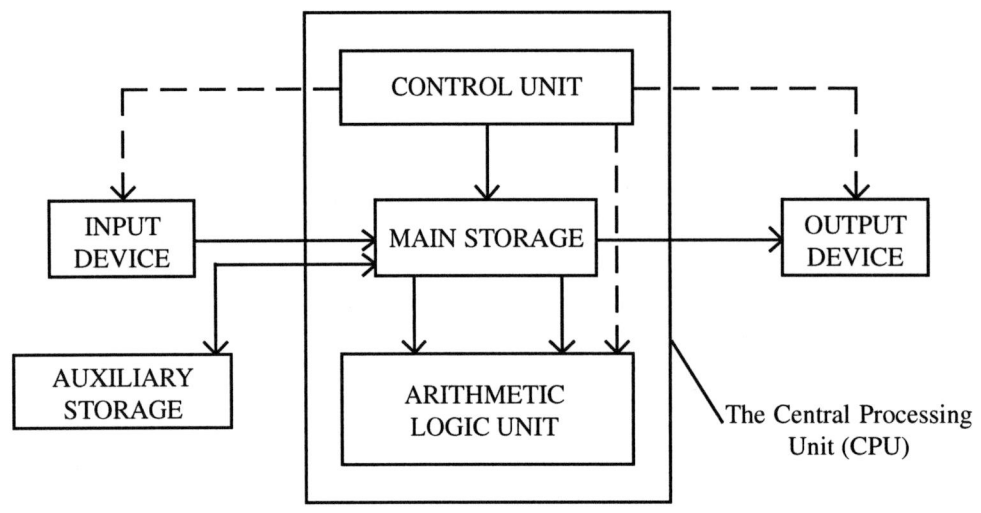

The computer needs a device for the input of instructions to allow the human operator to 'talk' to the computer. Similarly, the output device transmits the answers and information from the processes back to the user.

The items that carry out the processes are located so that they interact. The full lines on the diagram illustrate the movement of instructions and data and the dotted lines the routes of command signals.

It is now possible to locate the input and output devices thousands of miles away from the Central Processing Unit or CPU and to use telephone lines or satellites to provide the communication links.

If we consider a microcomputer on a desk, the keyboard is the input device, the screen the output device and the CPU would be located in a large box (called the system box). The disk drive for the insertion of a floppy disk provides the facility for auxiliary storage.

This set up would enable a user to carry out all the necessary processing.

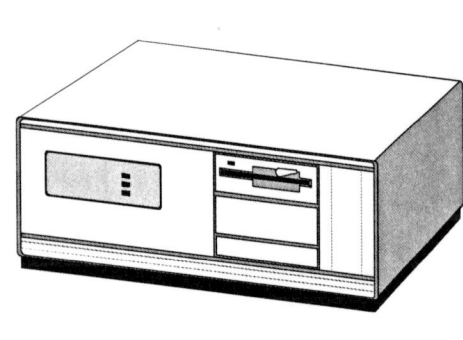

The CPU lies within the main system box known as the computer.

Peripheral devices are connected to the computer to provide alternative facilites for input or output. Printers and scanners would come into this category. Most processes still require all or some of the output to be on paper and so most computers are connected to a printer either directly or through some form of shared switch.

Most offices are now equipped with desk top or microcomputers so the following descriptions of the various components relate to those items most likely to be seen in an office environment.

9.2 Input Devices

A   Keyboard

The keyboard is perhaps the most frequently used component for the entry of instructions and data to a stand alone microcomputer. The layout of a keyboard is based on the QWERTY design which originated on the typewriter. The alphabetic characters are placed in one block surrounded by a row of numeric and special characters.

The use of a combination of the shift and the relevant key provide capital letters and the special characters. A further set of numbers are arranged on the right of the keyboard in a similar fashion to that used on calculators. This is the numeric key pad. There is a row of twelve function keys at the top of the keyboard which are used by packaged software to provide various shortcuts in the processes they offer. Cursor control and navigation keys make up the remainder.

Special types of keyboards are available for left handed people, in which the cursor movement keys are located on the left hand side, and for people with physical disabilities.

The QWERTY Keyboard

During the 1980's, there was growing concern over the damage caused by the prolonged use of keyboards. Court cases were brought by employees against their employers for Repetitive Strain Injury (RSI) and some were successful in obtaining a financial settlement. It is now possible to obtain a wrist support which sits in front of the keyboard which should reduce the possibility of strain.

Microsoft have produced a 'natural keyboard', the layout of which follows the description above but the keyboard is curved to provide a more normal position for the hands.

In some commercial situations 'concept keyboards' are used in which each of the keys represents a particular item that the business sells. These are used to input information at cash tills in fast food restaurants and public houses. Pressing a key pad is detected by the software and interpreted into the item sold. The computer system 'looks up' the price of the item and transmits the data to the cash till. The user does not need to memorise a long list of prices.

B   Mouse

The use of icons and pulldown menus allows the users to make their choices and issue instructions much faster. To maximise the use of these techniques a high resolution pointing device has been developed called the mouse.

An arrow shaped cursor is displayed on the screen and by moving the mouse on a table top the arrow can be located where needed on the screen. Once the required object on the screen has been found the user presses or 'clicks ' a button on the body of the mouse to make a selection. The software converts the co-ordinates of the arrow and carries out the required instruction. This form of interaction between the user and the computer is known as 'point and click'. This form of input is very quick and simple to use but it requires sufficient room on the desk adjacent to the computer for the movement of the mouse.

C   Tracker or Roller Ball

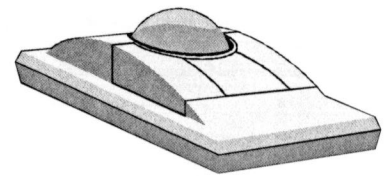

In laptop computers where space is restricted, similar functions are carried out by a tracker ball. This device consists of a ball, mounted in a fixed position in a frame. Rotating the ball moves the arrow around the screen. On the mounting frame are a number of buttons so that the user's choices can be confirmed.

Neither of the above two devices can enable data to be placed in a data entry screen. They can only be used to select one of a number of options displayed on a screen.

D Bar Code Reader

Almost any item of data can be represented by a bar code. Two main coding systems in use are the Universal Product Code (UPC) and the European Article Number (EAN). The row of different thickness black and white stripes is perhaps more familiar on items on the shelves of a shop where they can be interpreted to give information on the country of origin, manufacturer or maker, and a description of the item.

It is possible to encode people's names and other forms of data. They are useful because they allow data to be read directly into the computer and the process is both quick and accurate. Some readers are in the form of a light pen or wand which is wiped across the bar pattern. The code signals generated by the pattern of lines are decoded by special software and the data transmitted to the computer. The code can be wiped in either direction with the same results. More robust hand-held readers are used in situations that require a more mobile device.

A Light Pen Bar Code Reader

Software is available to print the bar code labels to any specification. These labels are usually printed on laser or high quality printers.

E Scanner, Digitiser and Digital Camera

A digitiser is a device for converting pictures into a digital image suitable for storing in a computer or displaying on a computer screen. The pictures are converted into a set of small dots, called pixels.

A digital camera digitises a visual image and stores it as a still picture on a magnetic storage device. The camera looks like and is the same size as a normal photographic camera. The digital pictures can be loaded into a computer for storage and display.

A scanner is a device for converting an image on paper into a digitised form for use by a computer. The scanner reads the image on the paper, converts it into a set of pixels and stores the image in a computer file. This image can be altered and imported into a document and then printed. Text on paper can be read as an image and then converted into a computer text document using optical character reading software.

F Microphone

This is a small device similar to those used with audio equipment which stores sound digitally on a computer.

G   Joystick

A joystick is used to move a cursor around a screen and is most commonly used with games playing software.   The user can operate the joystick, for instance, to target images and direct "gunfire".

9.3 Output Devices

A   The Visual Display Unit (VDU) or Monitor

This is probably the most common output device.   The standard PC screen measures 15 inches across the diagonal, although now screens of 17 and 19 inches are common.   The new versions of software require the use of colour monitors.   Technology has fortunately reduced the cost of these to the same level as a monochrome or single colour screen. It is possible to dislay 256 colours on a screen.   The screen area is divided into a number of pixels and the higher the number of these, the higher the resolution of the screen.

Present common standards are VGA 640 pixels X 480 pixels, and SVGA 800 pixels X 600 pixels. The displayed picture is regenerated a number of times per second, called the **refresh rate**, although the image appears to be constant when viewed by the human eye.   There are various methods of creating the screen displays.

Certain applications such as desk top publishing (DTP) require the use of high resolution and larger screens so that a full page can be displayed and edited on the screen.

B   Printers

Despite the fact that the data is stored electronically there is still a demand for obtaining hard or paper copy of documents.   There are a number of different forms of printer available on the market that use different means to imprint the information on the paper. The various printer mechanisms create different quality of output and hence the price of the device.

Dot Matrix Printers

In this type of printer the characters are created by a series of wires or pins that are pushed forward in the desired pattern and are impacted onto the ribbon which is then pressed onto the paper. The number of strikes required to create the full image of the character depends on the size of the matrix used for the representation. The ascenders and descenders can easily be accommodated.

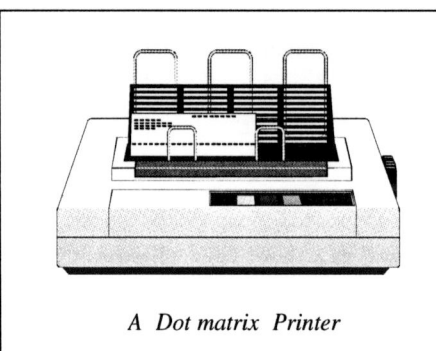

A Dot matrix Printer

Ascenders are letters which extend above the line of text such as h or k.

Descenders are letters which extend below the line of text such as g, p or q.

To create the character in the diagram left, the print head would contain a vertical column of 7 wires and the full character would appear after the head had completed four strike positions. In each position different combinations of wires are pressed against the paper. An examination of the printout will reveal that each character is produced from an assembly of small dots. Obviously a larger matrix provides a smoother easier to read character. This type of printer is used to provide low quality fast copy and is suitable for program listings and draft documents. It is possible, because this is a **percussion or impact printer**, to use carbon paper to produce more than one copy at a time.

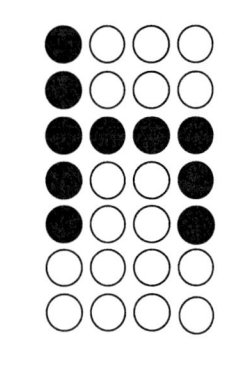

A *percussion printer* is one that produces its characters by a striking action.

The quality of the printed image is described in terms of its **resolution**, e.g. high resolution or low resolution. The resolution is measured in **dots per inch** or **dpi**. The higher the resolution, i.e. the greater the number of dots per inch, the greater the quality of image.

Ink Jet Printer

The ink jet printer produces characters of a very high quality. The ink is stored in cartridges which have nozzles that can direct electrically charged ink particles to form the characters on the paper. Many models can hold colour cartridges and produce excellent colour output. The output can be laid onto paper or when necessary an overhead projector (OHP) transparency. This form of printer is ideal for business letters, for the preparation of presentation documents and all situations in which high quality output is a requirement.

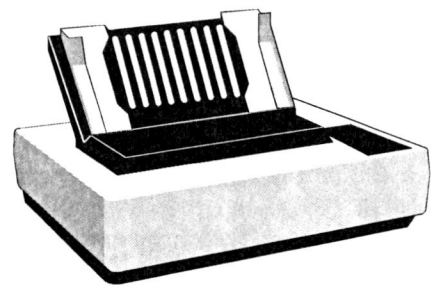

Laser Printers

When this type of printer was first introduced it was extremely expensive but with its high quality of output, it has become very popular and its price has been drastically reduced. Laser printers are now more affordable. The laser printer has always been classified as a page printer. The images are printed using a high intensity laser and an electrophotographic technique similar to that used in photocopiers.

An electrical charge is applied to a drum coated with a photoconductive material which is selectively discharged by a laser beam leaving an electrically charged image of the page to be printed. Passing this through a toner enables the image to be transferred from the drum to the paper. The quality of the output is extremely high, close to that obtainable in the printing industry and now that the price has dropped, this quality is available even to small businesses. The output is produced quickly and the printers make very little noise.

C   Plotters

Plotters are available in two main types:-

Flat Bed Plotters

The paper lies flat on a bed and a set of ink pens moves across the paper to create the image. The pens are mounted on a carriage and by a combination of the movement of the carriage across the paper and the pens along the carriage all the various shapes can be printed. Colour pens can be included to enhance the image. This type of plotter is available in various paper sizes.

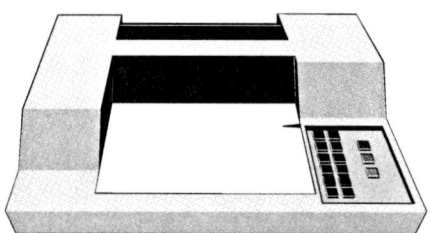

Drum Plotter

The paper is attached around a drum and attached to sprocket wheels at each side. The pens are mounted in a carriage that is fixed across the paper the full width of the drum and the pens have the ability to move across the carriage. This provides movement in only one direction. The paper is moved backwards and forwards to create the other form of movement needed to create the shapes and images.

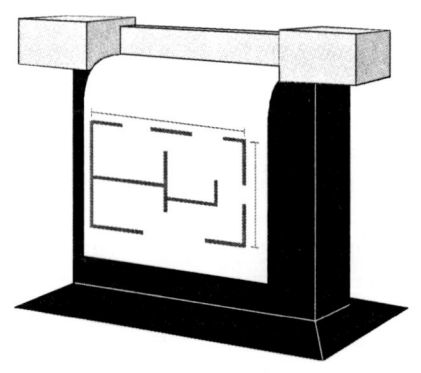

This type of plotter can also draw the diagrams in colour and can operate with very large sheets of paper.

D   Loudspeaker

Modern microcomputer sytems can produce sound as well as visual and printed images. To achieve this, a sound card is added to the computer and a pair of small loudspeakers. This enables the user to use software with a sound output, play music and receive sound over the Internet.

9.4 The Central Processing Unit (CPU)

The diagram to the right shows the Central Processing Unit (CPU).

It has three main components,
the **Control Unit**,
the **Arithmetic Logic Unit**
and **Main Storage**.

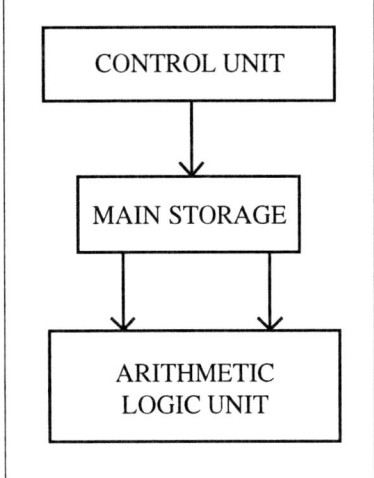

A   The Control Unit

The control unit acts like the conductor of an orchestra ensuring that all of the other components including the input and output devices carry out their functions correctly. It 'fetches' each instruction, interprets its meaning and oversees its execution. It is electronically linked to all of the other components so that it can detect if the required device or component is connected, ensure that the device is aware and ready to carry out the instruction and in the absence of the device, arrange to display an error message on the screen to alert the operator.

B   The Arithmetic/Logic Unit (ALU)

All mathematical calculations and operations such as addition, subtraction, multiplication and division are carried out by the ALU. The Items of data to be the subject of the calculations are temporarily transferred to the ALU, the operations performed and the answers returned to main storage.

It is also used to make 'logical' comparisons, many of which will determine the route taken through a program. For instance a particular routine may only be called if the value of a particular variable is equal to zero. The value of the variable held in storage will be transferred to the ALU, its value compared with zero and the reply transmitted back to main storage.

C Main Storage

The Main Storage of the machine strores all of the data to be processed. The items are entered from an input device. This could be a component such as a keyboard or even another storage device such as a diskette containing a data file. The data will reside in memory while it is processed. It will then be joined by the results of the processing, which will be held until it is transferred to an output device.

Also resident in this area will be the program that is responsible for the processing.

Main storage provides the processor with fast access to the information it requires. The various processes that are undertaken require different facilities to be available for the storage of the data and program instructions. Therefore, there are various types of memory, the most common of which are **ROM**, Read Only Memory, and **RAM**, Random Access Memory.

Random Access Memory (RAM)

It is possible to read and write to this form of memory but its contents will be deleted when the power is turned off so it is described as being 'volatile'. This is the area in which the programs and the items of data that are being processed will be held while the operations are being carried out. The size of this type of storage determines the speed at which the programs operate and some of the packages now available require a high level of RAM to make their use effective. When preparing a specification for the purchase of a computer the establishment of the quantity of RAM required will be a major factor.

Read Only Memory (ROM)

This type of memory will contain pre-defined program instructions that are written permanently onto the device during manufacture. These instructions are unaffected by switching off or the loss of power so it is said to be 'non-volatile'.

In many computers an area of **cache memory** is included in the specification. Many of the devices used for storage, such as disk drives, operate at a slower speed than the processor. The components that make up the cache provide the facility of fast access speeds and are inserted between the processor and the slower devices.

The contents are eventually overwritten as processing continues. The size of the cache provided will determine how long each item is present and how quickly they become overwritten.

Cache Memory

This provides a temporary storage for the items most recently processed from which the items can be retrieved faster and more readily.

Storage Capacity

Computer storage capacity is measured in terms **bytes**. The smallest data item stored in a computer is a binary digit called a **bit**. A byte is eight bits in size and can store a character such as a letter or punctuation mark. A thousand bytes is called a **kilobyte** and a million bytes is called a **megabyte** or **Mbyte**. A thousand megabytes is called a **gigabyte** or **Gbyte**. A thousand gigabytes is called a **terabyte**.

These are, in fact, close approximations: a kilobyte is in fact 1024 bytes or 2^{10} bytes, a megabyte is 1,048,576 or 2^{20} bytes, a gigabyte is 1,073,741,824 or 2^{30} bytes and a terabyte is 1,099,511,627,776 or 2^{40} bytes

Microcomputers bought today, commonly have 64 megabytes of internal memory and many have 128 or 256 megabytes.

D   Types of Processor

In microcomputers the control unit and arithmetic/logic unit are held on one chip called the processor and the main storage on many chips; the more memory, the more chips.

There continues to be a constant need to develop and install processors that are capable of carrying out the operations faster and in larger quantities. The processor is the hardware component that converts the input data into output information according to a pre-defined set of instructions. The action of the processor is initiated by a 'clock' that is ticking continuously and depending on the complexity of the instruction the action will continue for one or more 'clock ticks'. The speed at which the clock ticks can be used to specify the speed of the processor. The higher the speed will mean that the processor can deal with a larger number of operations in the same time.

A clock rate of 600Mhz means that the clock ticks once every 1/600,000,000 second. Processors have traditionally been numbered with the first digit representing the generation from which it comes. Thus a 386 processor is a third generation chip and a 486 processor is a fourth generation chip.

With the advent of the fifth generation called a **Pentium** this practice has been discontinued. It is possible to purchase processors of the same generation but which operate at different clock speeds.

9.5 Auxiliary Storage

This storage area, provided in much larger quantities than any other type of storage, contains much of the software and data used for and produced as a result of processing. It is separate from the CPU. It does not operate as fast as main storage and the recorded information will be retained when the power is switched off.

The devices used for this type of storage have their roots in the music industry and have developed from reel-to-reel tape to cassettes, disks and now CD's. Modern desk top computers use a number of types of disk to provide this facility.

A   Floppy Disks

These are in the form of a circular sheet of material coated on both sides with a recording medium. This is encased in a hard plastic container to protect the material and the information stored on it. Over the years, manufacturers have been able to reduce the size of the disks and yet increase the amount of data that can be stored on them. The current standard now appears to be the the 3.5 inch diameter disk. The amount of data that can be stored will be determined by the density at which the data items are packed on to the disk.

Before use, the disks have to be formatted or marked out magnetically. This process divides the storage area into a number of sectors, normally nine, and then to 'scribe' the tracks. These are concentric circles into which the data will be recorded. There will generally be 80 tracks on each side of the disk so when the process is complete the disk will contain 720 addressable locations on each side. During the formatting process the **Directory** track will also be created in which an index of the contents of the disk will be stored. Once the data has been recorded, the write tag can be used to prevent the contents being overwritten.

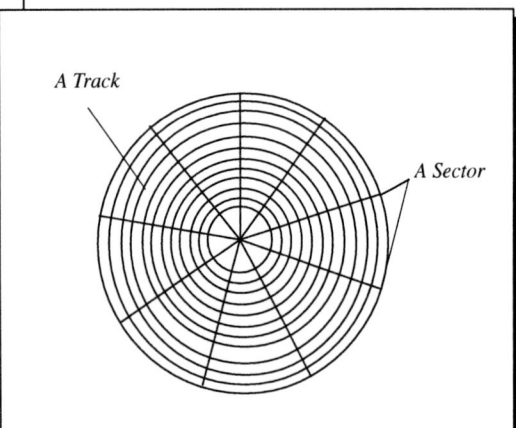

These disks do not operate as fast as the other types but they provide a cheap and transportable storage medium and in recent years they have become increasingly secure.

B   Hard Disks

Hard disks are manufactured in metal and coated with a magnetisable recording medium. They are housed in a sealed unit to prevent damage from dust and other air-borne matter. They are located inside the computer system unit which is the main box that holds the central processing unit. The recorded information can be accessed much faster and transferred much quicker. Depending on the storage capacity of the unit, it may comprise a number of disks each having its own read/write head. Whilst providing a secure means of storing data and programs, it is advisable to copy the contents onto some other device in case a catastrophe corrupts the recorded information.

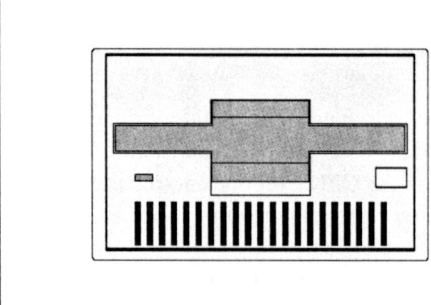

C   CD ROM

Compact Disk Read Only Memory, sometimes referred to as an optical disk, is an ideal device for storing large quantities of information and data such as large software packages, encyclopaedias, and other forms of data that are used for reference. The CD drive uses laser technology to read the disk contents and therefore both access and transfer are extremely fast. The disks can store all types of data including pictures, drawings and music. With the increasing growth in the size of the commercial software packages, they are now being supplied on this type of medium.

D   Digital Versatile Disk (DVD)

Digital Versatile Disk is a new type of CD-ROM. It is the same size as a CD-ROM but is double-sided: data is stored on both sides of the disk.   DVD technology uses a very shortwave laser beam to read pits from the spining disk. The technology used for video is called MPEG-2 and for audio is AC-3. If you wish to have a DVD drive in your computer, a decoding card is needed.

DVD's are used to deliver movies and music.   A standard DVD holds 4.7 Gbytes of data.

There are three types of DVD drives which are:

read only   Data is recorded on the disk when it is pressed.

recordable   These are known as "write once" disks.   They are supplied blank and data can be recorded once on them.   The format for these is DVD-R.

rewritable   These can be re-used thousands of times.   They are written in several incompatible formats, including:

    DVD+RW used by Sony and Hewlett Packard.

    DVD-RAM used by Toshiba and Hitachi.

9.6 Backup Storage Devices

It is vital that all files stored in a computer system are backed up regularly. There is so much work done on computers today that, in most cases, backing up to a normal floppy disk is not appropriate: it can store only 1.44 Megabytes of data. For single machines, a number of devices are available for backup.

These include, at the time of writing this book:

Cartridge tape back-up drives, which can hold up to 10 Gigabytes on a single tape. A single micro-computer is likely to use a 1 or 2 Gigabyte drive.
Zip disk drives, which store 100 Megabytes of data on a single disk.
Jaz disk drives, which hold 1 or 2 Gigabytes on a single disk.
SyQuest disk drive, which holds up to 1.5 Gigibytes on a single disk.
High capacity super floppy disk drives which can hold up to 120 Megabytes on a single disk.
CD writers, which hold 680 Megabytes of storage on a single disk.

The disk storage drives are faster than the tape drives, but at present the tapes hold more data.

 Activity 9.1

Collect information from a number of PC magazines and produce a catalogue of printers. Include a description of each printer along with its price.

 Activity 9.2

Collect information about PC storage devices and for each write a description of its advantages and disadvantages.

Chapter 10
Software

Objectives

At the end of this chapter you will be able to describe

- [ ] the operating system
- [ ] a graphics user interface
- [ ] applications software
- [ ] configuration of the system
- [ ] the types of application software
- [ ] configuring applications software
- [ ] operating system and application software testing

10.1 Introduction

The computer cannot run without special programs called **software**. There are two types of software that we will be concerned with, which are:

System Software

This is the set of programs that run the computer. It includes the operating system. Most micro-computers that students in schools and colleges will use are those developed from the IBM PC. These use the DOS operating system and Windows. The operating system environments with which most students will have familiarity, are Windows 95, 98 and 2000. Windows 2000 was launched earlier this year.

Systems software such as Windows 2000 use a **graphics user interface** to present information to and receive information from a user. This includes clear illuminated screens with graphic images to represent systems and applications software. The user issues commands to the system by pointing with a cursor driven by a hand-held mouse.

Applications software

This is software that is concerned with what the computer is used for. Computers are used to create documents, such as letters, reports and posters. This is called word processing. Word processing is an **application** of the computer and word processing software is an example of **applications software**. Spreadsheet and database software are futher types of applications software.

Applications software can be bought off-the-shelf, e.g. Microsoft Office 2000, or can be written using a programming language.

10.2 The Operating System

An Operating System (OS) is a set or suite of programs created to optimise the use of the computer. The most common operating system used in microcomputers is MS-DOS (Microsoft Disk Operating System). The act of switching the computer on initiates the running of a program which will test that the components are functioning and which will be completed with the display of the system prompt to make the user aware that the machine is now ready for work. If the name of a program is entered at this time the OS will arrange for the program to be loaded into the correct area of main storage. An area will be set aside for the data generated by the program and when necessary the OS will arrange for the data to be transferred into the ALU for processing and for the return of the answers on completion. The operating system will control the direction of data to and from the correct input and output devices and produce a warning when the required device is not connected or the transfer has failed. This will include transfers to and from auxiliary storage and printers.

System Prompt

C:\\>

This is a system prompt indicating that the C drive is current.

The term **file** is used to describe any output that is stored on a storage device. This may include the data stored for a particular application, a program or, on many occasions a document created using a wordprocessor.   When access to the stored information is required the relevant file has to be opened and on completion of the operation, once any data has been written back to the file, it will then be closed. These file operations are also carried out by the operating system. The titles or names of all of the files stored on a device are recorded in a **folder**, sometimes called a **directory**.   Another operation carried out by the operating system is the **maintenance** of the directory.

*A **Folder** is a location in which you can store a set of files and/or folders.   It can also be considered as a list of the files that are stored on a storage device or part of a storage device.   The list will include the file names, the size of each file and the time and date when the file was last saved.   The term directory also refers to the files that are listed and grouped together.*

***Maintenance** This means maintaining or keeping the directory in good order. New files are added to the directory and unwanted ones removed.*

Operating systems provide a language with a limited vocabulary to enable user routines to be developed. One of the uses of the language included in MS-DOS is for the development of a **batch program**. When the computer is switched on and the checking routines are complete the OS will search the directory for the presence of a batch program and if it finds one it will automatically run it.   Such a program could be written to display a particular screen layout at the beginning of processing to perhaps list for the user the names of the application programs that are available.   This is known as providing a **front end**.

The systems software will also include a number of routines necessary for the organisation of the storage medium and the data it contains. A routine will be provided for the formatting of disks, a process that has already been described. Further routines will allow for the creation, maintenance and deletion of sub-directories. Therefore the storage of data can be arranged so that the user can create a type of filing cabinet on the disk and keep like items together. For instance the output from a word processor will consist of reports, letters, and miscellaneous items such as notices and posters. A **sub-directory** can be set aside for storing each of the types of documents. Alternatively, it might be more sensible for the directories to refer to the names of the recipients of the documents. Either way the facility regularises the storage of the data and simplifies access to the files.

> ### *Sub-Directory*
>
> *When a directory of files is divided into different groups each group is called a sub-directory.*

10.3 Graphics User Interface

A graphics user interface (GUI) provides a more friendly environment for the user. It provides brightly lit screens, icons, windows, drop-down menus, buttons and rulers.

Each icon represents a task and if it is selected by pointing and clicking with the left mouse button, the associated task will be carried out. The act of selection causes software to be run that will carry out the desired task. The Microsoft Windows screens provide the most familiar graphics user interface.

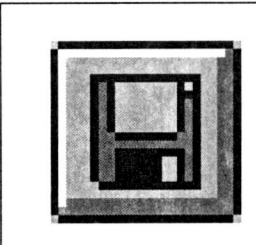

A Save ICON

A Package ICON

Graphics user interfaces enable the user to manage both system and application tasks without understanding how many of the tasks are achieved. Users can format disks, look after the files stored on the disks, change a number of the physical details of the screen display and specify the interaction of the computer and any peripheral device to which it is connected.

Applications can be loaded and once in place the operations included in the application can also be initiated in the same way, normally by selecting the required option from a list in a **drop-down menu**.

Applications packages use similar screen formats with similar instructions located in the same place. This provides a form of comfort for the user and increases their familiarity with Windows-based packages.

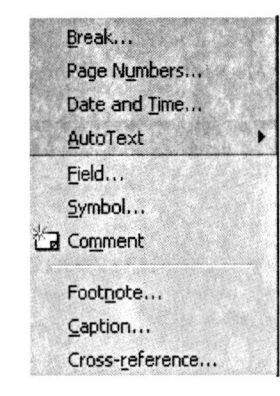

A Drop Down Menu

10.4 Applications Software

Applications software programs can be :-

written and developed using a programming language,
bought as a commercially available package, or
developed using the facilities of a commercially available package.

A   Programming Languages

When computers were first introduced the program instructions were strings of binary digits and programmers had to provide details of the functions to be performed and the storage areas to be used for the various values used in the processes.

This type of language is a **machine language**.

In a machine language, a program code for writing a value might be represented as

instruction	memory location
1010	10010011

You can see that it was very difficult to work in binary - pages and pages of 0s and 1s are hard to read. Because of this **assembly languages** were introduced that used a series of mnemonics to represent the instructions and names to represent the memory locations. The instruction above might become

WTE   LENGTH

*A **mnemonic** is a set of characters that helps you to think of the meaning of something. In the above case WTE represents write.*

With assembly languages it was still necessary to maintain a knowledge of the **memory map** to be aware of the whereabouts of each of the stored values.

These were known as **low level languages** because they were **machine-oriented**.

*A **memory map** is the arrangement of data stored in the main memory of the computer.*

***Machine-oriented** means that the languages were individual to each type of computer so the machine or assembly language of one manufacturer would not run on a computer made by another manufacturer.   They had a strong relationship to the hardware.*

With the growth of computers, **high level languages** were introduced to enable programs to be written to solve commercial problems. The instructions were prepared using a normal vocabulary such as read, write, print and input, and mathematical operators such as = , + and -.

However, the computers still want their instructions in machine code so, once completed, the programs are converted into binary representation using a piece of software called a **compiler or interpreter**. During this process the storage addresses of each of the **variables** is allocated.

> *A <u>variable</u> is a name that can take on a value during the processing, e.g. length.*

These languages were aimed at particular sectors of business and technical situations. Examples are:

COBOL (Common Business Oriented Language). This contains many facilities for the presentation of information but is not very useful for carrying out difficult calculations and hence it is used to generate code for business solutions.

FORTRAN (Formula Translation) is more suitable for scientific applications as it is ideally suited for carrying out complex mathematical problems but does not concentrate on presentation.

With the advent of the home computer, **BASIC** (**B**asic **A**ll Purpose **S**ymbolic **I**nstruction **C**ode) became very popular and still exists along with **Pascal** as a language that is easier to learn and can be used to generate programs for a number of applications. These are known as **third generation languages.**

Many **fourth generation languages** have been around for some years. They enable a program to be constructed using less lines of instruction to achieve the same operations as their predecessors and so they have a **programming productivity** over COBOL of at least 10:1. Programs are slow to execute and they require powerful processors. The individual languages are accompanied by different **software tools** some of which generate the code to create the processes declared by the programmer but most include facilities for report writing, data description, screen painting and file handling.

> *<u>Software tools</u> are programs that the programmer can use to carry out tasks that help build programs.*

> *<u>Programming productivity</u> tells you about the efficiency of a language. It tells you how much program can be written with a given number of lines of program. If it takes ten lines to write a program in language A and 100 lines to achieve the same result in language B then language A has a programming productivity of 10 to 1 or 10:1 over language B.*

Using any of these high level languages, a program can be written from an agreed specification to provide for the exact requirements of a particular application. Such a system is called **bespoke**. A bespoke system requires a very detailed specification and description of the problem and a well thought out test plan to ensure that it will cope with all of the possible input values and errors that may occur during processing. Producing a program in this way would probably take longer. Amendments and improvements to the program would be easier.

B   Commercial Software

It is possible to purchase a ready made, off-the-shelf **generic** solution to most commercial problems.

*These are called **generic** packages because they are written for general use by a wide range of users.*

*A **compromise** is made when something has to be sacrificed to use the package, e.g. you may want the package to store two phone numbers for a customer instead of one but the package may not allow it. You make a compromise if you accept this limitation.*

Unfortunately, because the package has been designed to be used by a number of different types of organisation, its facilities will usually never quite fit a particular situation. This may require a **compromise** to be made. A decision has to be made as to how much of a compromise the user is prepared to make.

A software licence has to be purchased in order to use a package. Such a licence will refer to the number of copies that can be in use at any one time. Illicit copying of the software is an offence punishable in law. Any purchaser should be sure about the capabilities of the package before obtaining it and to cost the implications of such a purchase. It may well be necessary to replace all of the printed stationary within the organisation to fit the requirements of the package and this item alone could be prohibitive. Packages provide a fast solution to problems. Keeping the packages up-to-date is the responsibility of the package producer. Updated packages may be supplied through the licence agreement or a maintenance agreement.

C   Adapting Commercial Software

Many of the generic packages are now accompanied by a form of programming language which allows for the package to be **customised** to fit more closely the needs of the organisation purchasing it. The use of **macros** is discussed later in this book. This could make the purchase of a package a more likely solution but does require having someone that understands the language, to provide an efficient solution and to maintain the program so that it can absorb changes in the processes that will evolve from its use.

***Customising** is the process of making the package suit the user's needs, e.g. by allowing a second customer telephone number in the example above.*

10.5 Configuring the System

The operating system can be used to configured the system to meet the needs of the user. These include:

setting time and date,
organising the desktop,
setting passwords,
organising the structure of folders and files,
setting the display,
configuring the mouse, and
carrying out anti-virus checks.

Setting Time and Date

Facilities are available to set the time and date. For instance in Windows this is done through the Control Panel. Settings are made using the Date/Time Properties dialog box.

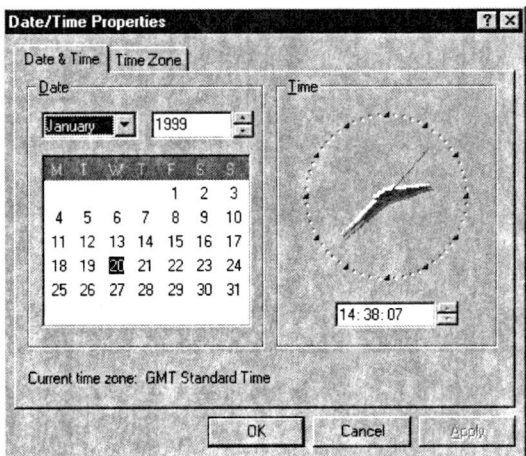

Organising the Desktop

The Windows environment consists of a **desktop**, **menus** and a number of **windows**. When you work on your computer all your activities take place in windows; a window being a rectangular area of the screen. You may run one application, say, a word processor in one window, and another application, perhaps a database system, in a different window.

The tasks that you are currently running are held on the **Taskbar**, usually at the bottom of your desktop. The desktop holds icons for some of the programs that are available to you. Some of your software can be accessed through the Programs menu. You have the choice of whether to display the software icons or have them only on the Programs menu.

The desktop icons can be moved around the desktop and the Taskbar can be moved to the side.

Organising Folders and Files

The Window operating system uses a software program, Windows Explorer, to help you organise and maintain your files, which may be on your hard disk or your floppy disk. To run the Windows Explorer, click on the name in the Programs menu. This will produce a window showing disc drives, folders and files. The left hand side of the window shows folders and the right hand side shows the contents of the selected folder on the left hand side.

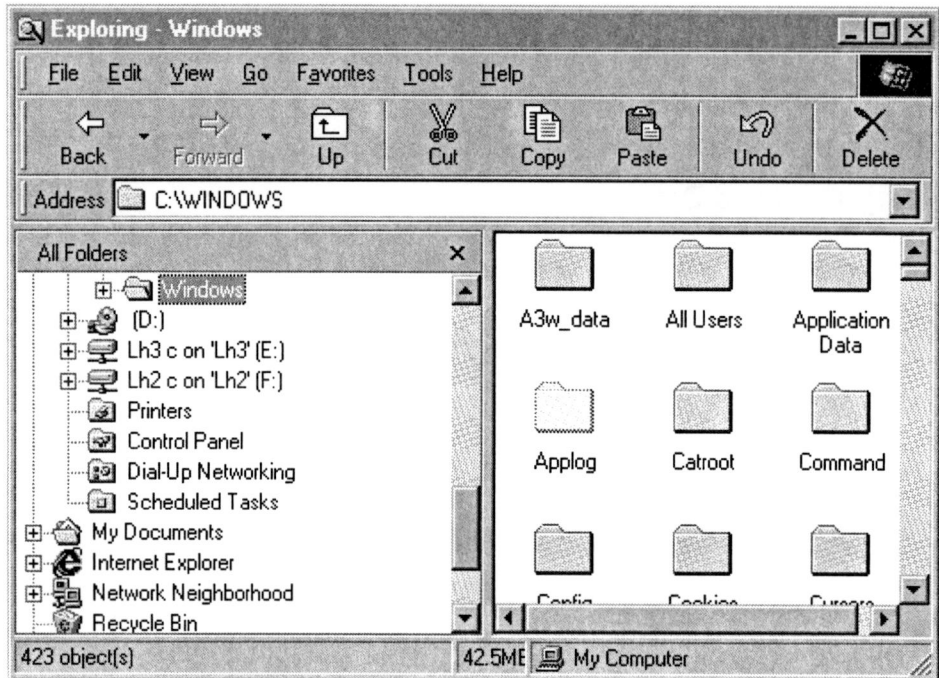

Selections can be made by double-clicking on the items on the right hand side of the window or by clicking on the arrow in the drop-down list box at the top left of the window and selecting with a single click from the list produced. A click on desktop shows the top level structure of the desktop.

Files and folders can be moved, copied and deleted using this facility.

Setting the Display

In Windows, display settings, such as screen resolution, background, screen server and screen colour, can be altered through the Display Properties dialog box which can be displayed through the Control Panel or by right-clicking on the desktop and selecting Properties.

The Mouse

The Mouse Properties dialog box can also be displayed through the Control Panel. This allows the mouse buttons and pointer speed to be configured.

Setting Passwords

In Windows, sytem passwords can also be set through the Control Panel and the Passwords Properties dialog box.

Initiating Anti-Virus Checks

It is very important to protect your computer from viruses. To do this, anti-virus software has to be installed. Once done, it can be used to check any of the storage devices on your computer system using a command from the operating system.

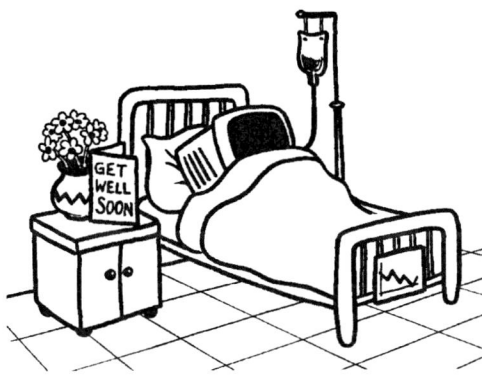

10.6 Types of Application Software

In this Unit, you need to be familiar with the different types of application software, so that you can satisfy users needs. You need to be familiar with:

word processing,
desktop publishing,
database management,
spreadsheets,
graphics,
programming languages,
utilities,
calendars and diaries, and
e-mail.

Word Processing

Computers are used for producing letters, reports, newsletters and other text documents. A user will type a letter into the computer and when it is finished it will be printed on to paper. This is a job that is very often done by computers and is called **word processing**. Word processing is a computer application.

Wordprocessors are very good at creating documents that are mainly words. They can check the spelling of words and how they are used. They can change the appearance of words on a page and can produce very attractive layouts.

There are many benefits of wordprocessors. They are very **productive**. This means that they can produce many copies of a letter or other document very quickly. Before the use of wordprocessors, if a person wanted to send a copy of a letter to many customers, each one would have to be typed separately with a different address on each. If a mistake was made, the page would have to be typed again.

With a wordprocessor, one letter can be typed and a special facility, called **mail merging**, is available to allow it to be printed many times and sent to any number of people without any need to type further letters. Each letter has the name and address added for each person to whom the letter is to be sent. The names and addresses are held on a data file, which can be used over and over again for different letters.

If a mistake is made, it can be corrected in the computer and the letter reprinted. Modern wordprocessors have many different types of lettering, called fonts, so **more attractive** letters can be produced.

Desk Top Publishing

Desk top publishing brings together the power of word processing and graphics and adds a range of new facilities. Traditionally wordprocessors created text documents suitable for business use. Graphics software allowed for the creation of pictures and drawings in both black and white and colour.

Desk top publishing software allowed the text documents to be brought together with the graphics to produce professional documents such as newspapers, journals and advertisements. Desk top publishing allowed for the creation of columns and for the placing of photographs and other graphic images at different positions on the page. The pictures could be rotated, scaled up or down and the final product was suitable for passing to a printer for the final production of the document.

Today, word processing software such as Microsoft Word, offers many of the facilities that desk top publishing packages provide.

A desk top publishing package organises it data in pages and handles text and pictures.

Database

Databases are used to store large amounts of data so that the user can obtain the information he or she needs when required and in an easy-to-understand form. They are **record-structured**. They allow the user to select the information required and to ignore the rest. Different users can use different parts of the database but may not be allowed to obtain the information from other parts.

The most common type of database is called a **relational database**. In this type of database, the data is held in tables and each **table** has a number of rows. An example of a table is shown below.

EMPLOYEE NUMBER	EMPLOYEE NAME	ADDRESS	TELEPHONE NUMBER
1000012	Brown A J	10, The High Street, Loadley	714536
1000043	Davis V C	4, Litten Terrace, Loadley	725776
1000085	Fowey J D	23, The Lane, Cumbley	562431
1000098	Northey A	43, Main Street, Lotton	345932

In most databases, there will be a number of tables, one for each type of item in the system. For example, there might be a table for customers, a table for suppliers, a table for products.

As well as the tables, the relationships between tables have to be defined. In other words, the relationship between products and suppliers and products and customers will be defined. This process links the tables together to form the complete database system. Hence the term **relational database.**

The software that manages the database is called a database management system. Access 2000 is a **relational database management system.**

Each row in the table above is called a **record**, in this case an employee record. Each item in the record is called a **field.**

Spreadsheet

Spreadsheet software is the most common software for organising and presenting numerical information. Spreadsheets are Number-Strucured Databases.

A spreadsheet is the electronic equivalent of a large sheet of paper and a calculator. It is divided up into columns and rows, making a large grid. Each element in the grid is called a **cell**, i.e. a cell is the place where a row and column cross.

Each column is given a letter and each row is given a number. Each cell, therefore, can be referred to by its column letter and row number. This is called its **cell reference**.

Spreadsheet software has the facility to present data in the form of charts. Microsoft Excel does this quite simply by allowing the user to highlight the data to be included in a chart and providing a set of steps which create a chart from the highlighted data.

Graphics

Graphics are pictures and drawings, stored in the computer as a set of pixels in a file. These files can be purchased as photo art or **clip art** on a CD ROM.

The graphics files can also be created from a photograph or a drawing using a **scanner**. This piece of equipment passes light over the picture and the scanning software on the computer converts the image into a file of pixels which can be stored and later imported into documents.

It is also possible to use a digital camera to capture an image and transfer it to computer. This can then be placed in a document using a desk top publishing package or wordprocessor.

When the picture has been created or imported it can be edited. This can be done using the scanning software after the picture has been created or in the desk top publishing package after it has been imported.

E-mail

Electronic mail is becoming a very common way for people to communicate with each other. It is the process of sending letters and documents over the Internet. It is now very easy to get a free E-mail account from a number of very high profile companies, such as Tesco, Freeserve and Virgin.

There are two different types of e-mail account.

If you have a dial-up Internet connection with an ISP, you will already have a pop3 e-mail account. To use it, you will need to use an E-mail client, e.g. Microsoft Outlook Express.

If you do not have an Internet account yourself, but have access to the Internet using somebody else's computer, you do not need to use Outlook Express. Instead you can open a web e-mail account.

10.7 Configuring Application Software

The application software may need to be configured to meet the needs of the user. The user may wish to accept the default settings in the software or may wish to have these settings specially altered. The alterations are reasonably simple and the user may wish to make these.

This configuration may include:

altering the layout of the software windows This may include altering the toolbar positions, the number of toolbars displayed, scroll bars, status bars and the buttons displayed on the toolbars.

altering or creating templates and macros The templates supplied with the software may need to be modified, e.g. to incorporate a logo. Macros may need to be written and be enacted using either a toolbar button or a menu item.

setting the folder and file structures The user may need to have folders and files created to handle the data. Sensible folder and filenames will need to be chosen.

adding and selecting printer drivers More than one printer may need to be configured. This will require the addiiotn of a number of printer drivers and selecting the default driver for each software package.

setting up file backup procedures Backup software may need to be loaded and parameters set. The frequency of backups will need to be established.

setting spelling an grammar checks Spelling and grammar checks may need to be set with the proper dictionaries and thesauruses.

10.8 Testing the Operating System and the Application Software

Once the operating system and application software has been loaded and configured to meet the needs of the user, it should be tested.

Testing means working through the operating system and the application software to check that each facility works. This will include:

powering up to check that the operating system loads properly and is ready for application software running,

and checking that:

the operating system is running properly   Some of this will be done when the application software is first loaded.

the applications will run   You will need to load each application program and run through its facilities.   You will need to check the menus and icons.

the macos work properly   It is important to check that the macros that you have created work well.   Use the macros on test data.

the templates are correct and print properly   Load each template, add the necessary addtional information and print it out.   Check that the document has no errors.

the files are accessible and that the file structure is correct   You will need to load the files for each software package and check that they are correctly located on the storage device.

the printers work well   You can carry out test printing to check the printers.

Activity 10.1

Load the operating system on your computer and make temporary changes. For example, alter the look of the desktop, alter the time and date, change the display properties and initiate an anti-virus check.

Activity 10.2

Load each major application program on your computer. Check the facilities available, create new files, check the printing and file structures.

Chapter 11
Computer Programming

Objectives

At the end of this chapter you will be able to describe

- computer programs
- HTML programs
- a web page publishing package
- web page design
- macro programming languages
- the facilities available for creating macros

11.1 Computer Programs

Computer programs are sets of logical instructions needed by the computer so that it can accept and process inputs and produce valid output.

You will already be familiar with application software, in the form of word processing, database, spreadsheets etc. The software which supports each of these is very complex and will have been designed by teams of programmers to meet the requirements of the specification given by the software manufacturer.

Most people who use computers will never need to write a computer program. Commercial application software offers all the facilities and features that most users need. Some organisations need special software that is not available on the market. They employ a software house or their own programmers to write the software they need.

You can see from the description of programming languages in Chapter 2, that programming is time-consuming. Before you embark on computer programming you need to:

produce a good specification of what you wish to achieve,
be sure that an off-the-shelf product is not avavailable, and
be able to write the program you need in a suitable programming language.

In this unit, you are not expected to write programs using traditional programming languages but you should become familiar with the purpose and facilities of:

hypertext mark-up language (HTML), and
macro programming languages.

You will not be expected to be able to write in these complex programming languages, but to use facilities such as wizards to produce the programming codes which make the process much easier.

11.2 HTML Programs

HTML is used to produce web pages and help pages in application software. It provides instructions to set up and lay out the pages to provide interest for the reader.

The basic template for all HTML documents is:

    <HTML>

        <HEAD>

        </HEAD>

        <BODY>

            The document itself goes here

        </BODY>

    </HTML>

The words surrounded by < and > are called **tags**. <HTML> and its closing tag </HTML> must surround the entire document.

    <HTML> should therefore always be the first line in every document and the last line should always be

    </HTML>

Each document should be divided into a HEAD and a BODY. The entire text for the web page is enclosed within the <BODY> and </BODY> tags. Liberty Hall's current home page is shown below.

Educational Publishers

Welcome To Liberty Hall's Home Page

Liberty Hall is an Educational Publishers who believe

books should be affordable and designed with the students in mind.

The HTML program code which produces this is:

```
<html>

<head>
<title>Home Page</title>
<meta http-equiv="Site-Enter" content="revealTrans(Duration=3.0,Transition=5">
</head>

<body bgcolor="#ffffff" link="#003311" alink="#003311" vlink #003311">

<centre><img src="images/liblogo.gif" width="265" height="113" alt="liblogo.gif (32064 bytes)" >

<BR><BR><BR><BR><BR>

<h1><font face="helvetica,arial">Welcome To Liberty Hall's Home Page</H1>

<BR></centre>

Liberty Hall is an Educational Publisher who believes that books should be affordable and designed with the stu
<BR><BR>
At Liberty Hall all our books have been written by good and experienced teachers who share our values.

<centre><BR><BR><BR>

<!-- BEGIN FASTCOUNTER CODE -->
```

You can see from the above that a number of tags and commands are used to produce the page. You can, if you wish, use a text processor to key in the programming language to produce the web page. You can use a wordprocessor such as Microsoft Word or a simpler package such as Notepad.

HTML programming software allows comments to be inserted, in the body of a program, to describe purpose of a section of the program code to anyone wishing to understand or modify the program.

11.3 Using a Web Page Publishing Package

There are a number of application packages available that will produce web pages without the need for the user to understand HTML. An example is Microsoft FrontPage 2000.

This package allows the user to place text and graphic objects on a web page, to link web pages together and publish the web pages on the internet. It uses wizards to speed up the process of web page creation and design. FrontPage will provide the HTML version of any web page created and it contains a browser so that the user can see the web pages as they will appear on the web.

In this unit, you are expected to be able to:

understand how hypertext systems operate. The previous sections have introduced you to this.

use web page software and wizards to create HTML-based pages. You need to have access to a package such as Microsoft FrontPage to gain experience of creating web pages using a wide range of web creation tools.

create hot spots Web page software will allow you to create image or text areas of the page that allow you to jump to other web pages on the Internet..

use a browser to view program pages To access the web, you will need to use a special software package. Microsoft Internet Explorer is the most commonly used browser in the world. You can view the HTML source code of a web page using Internet Explorer by accessing the web page and selecting **Source** from the **View** menu. The HTML will appear in a Notepad window.

make small modifications to HTML programs You will be expected only to alter text and add or remove a small number of tags.

11.4 Web Page Design

You are expected to be able to use a range of presentation techniques to improve the design of your web pages. Unit 1, *Presenting Information*, described a number of techniques. These included:

Planning your pages to suit the audience

You will need to design your web pages to suit the needs of the people you need to communicate with. The whole point of communication is to get a message across; the type of reader you are trying to attract will determine the style of the pages you produce. Remember that too much information is almost as bad at too little. It is very irritating for your audience to have to read through large blocks of text to extract just one or two points that concern them. The presentation and the language in which the document is written will need to change to meet the needs of the reader.

Planning your page structure

When you are creating you web pages it is important to plan the structure of each page beforehand. It is important that all your pages conform to a consistent style, using similar colours, font and font sizes. You will need to use the presentation techniques learned in Unit 1, such as:

Templates
Use of white space
Titles and headings
Fonts and sizes
Bold and italic text
Tables and tabs
Upper and lower case
Subscript and superscript
Graphics
Colour
Borders and shading
Bulleted lists
Justification
Columns
Special symbols
Headers and footers
Charts and graphs

Scanning and editing pictures

You may wish to include graphic images and pictures in a web page. One way of getting a picture or drawing into a form suitable for a web page is to digitise it. This can be done by using a scanner. The picture is placed in a scanner, a light source is passed slowly over it and the image is digitised. The scanning software will allow you to edit pictures.

The digitised image can be stored in a file on your computer. This image can then be imported into your web page using your web software.

Using Clip Art

Another way of adding images to your web page is to use clip art. This is a collection of images supplied by a business on a CD ROM, that can be used in text documents or web pages. Many software packages will import clip art for use in web pages.

Adding Sound Clips

It is possible to add sound to a web page, either as background sound to a page or as a sound effect when an action is taken. The sound is held in a sound file and is accessed using facilities in your web software, such as **Page Properties** in Microsoft FrontPage.

11.5 Macro Programming Languages

When computers were first produced, the software written for them was complicated and very detailed - see chapter 2. Every little step that the computer carried out had to be programmed. There were no graphics. Everything on screen was a sequence of numbers and letters displayed on a black background. The only people that could make the computer carry out its tasks were programmers.

As computers developed over the years, they became faster and the software more powerful. Today, Windows uses graphics to make the operation of the computer simpler and more attractive. Users, without programming expertise, can make the computer work in a range of diverse ways.

The trend over the past decades has been to make computers simple to use for users who do not have to know how computers work to use them. A single click on a button can make the computer carry out a task that requires many programming steps.

This process of carrying out an automatic sequence of actions with a single command is the basis of macro programming or macros (automated routines).

The main purposes of producing automated routines is to save time by minimising coding and to reduce errors to a minimum. By standardising procedures, especially if the procedure allows for input in a uniform format, not only does it save time but it produces a user-friendly environment.

Automatic routines can be anything from the simplest application software macro, e.g. inserting the current date and time by recording a macro; to the most complex of procedures called within computer programs.

How you record your macro will depend on the system and the application software. The examples given below use the Microsoft Office Suite of programs. If you do not have this software then look at the help menu of your software. Macros are quite easy to use.

11.6 The Facilities Available for Creating Automated Routines

The facilities which allow for automated routines include the following.

Macros As already explained, macros can be a very useful means of creating automated routines. In addition to creating templates to allow for standardisation, macros can be written and recorded to carry out calculations or to store and replicate large amounts of text if required. If used correctly macros can save an enormous amount of time and providing that the macro has been correctly recorded in the first instance you can be assured that it will reproduce accurately.

Batch files Batch files can be set up to hold large numbers of records in a uniform format. When the file is complete then the entire contents of the file can be processed at the same time by running a program which reads in each record in turn and, under a set of instructions written into the program, performs various processes in order that some form of output can be realised. Just what this output is will obviously depend on the program.

Examples of batch processing include employee wages. The batch file would be accessed either weekly or monthly by running a program which would calculate all of the employees' salaries and produce wage slips.

Programs Programs (sets of coded instructions) can perform any process required on data. As explained above, programs can be written to process batch files. Another type of program commonly used is inter-active programs, where the design of the program allows the user to respond to prompts given by the computer.

Example of a Microsoft Word Macro

The Task: Create and record a macro in Microsoft Word which allows for the date and time to be entered on the first line of your document. Assign a button so that each time it is pressed the date and time will appear.

In Word,
create a new document by clicking on **New File**,
click on **Tools** in the Menu bar,
select **Macro,**
choose **Record New Macro**.

This will produce the Record New Macro dialog box.

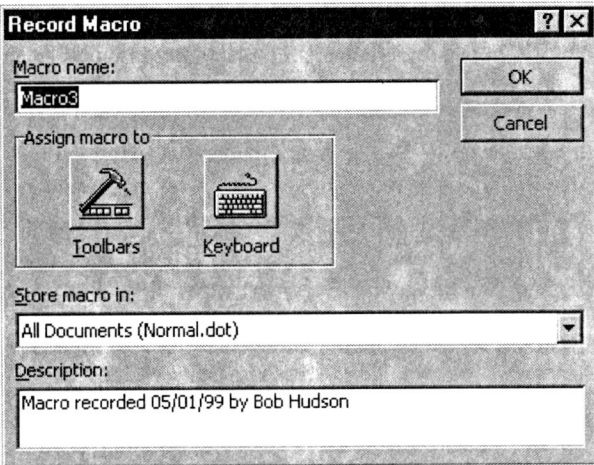

Enter the macro name **Datetime** and click on **OK**.

You will notice that a symbol with a Pause and Stop Button will appear - rather like that on a cassette recorder - if this is in the way move it down the page by dragging with the mouse.

Every command that you make will be recorded in the macro.

Leave the cursor right at the top of the new document.
Click on **Insert**.
Click on **Date and Time**. This will produce the Date and Time dialog box.
Select the format of date required, e.g. 05 January 2000.
Click on **OK**.
Click on the **STOP** button of the recorder.

To assign a button on the toolbar for this macro - click on **Tools** in the Menu bar.
Click on **Customise** to produce the Customise dialog box.
Click on the **Commands** tab.
Select **Macros** in the **Categories** list.
Select **Datetime** with the mouse and drag it up into the toolbar.
Click on **Close**.

Create a new file.
Click on the macro button you assigned and the date and time should appear.

 Activity 11.1

Create a macro to change the page layout by adjusting default settings for margins, page orientation; change the font style and size.

> *Remember, create a new document by clicking on **New File**, click on **Tools** in the Menu bar, select **Macro**, choose **Record New Macro**. Enter the macro name **Layout** in the Record New Macro dialog box and click on **OK**.*
>
> *Enter the commands necessary to set up the new page layout and click on the **STOP** button of the recorder.*

Activity 11.2

Create your own letter-headed paper. Each time you wish to write a letter you simply click on the appropriate macro button to bring the correct template up and type your letter.

Procedures are commonly used in programming. There are many benefits of using procedures to write programs. It saves an enormous amount of time and if you have problems in the execution of your program it is simple to track down where the problem is.

11.7 Using Wizards

Wizards are automated routines that allow the user to create a set of commands.
Microsoft Excel has a wizard to create a chart.

A click on the **Chart Wizard** button will produce the first Chart Wizard dialog box.

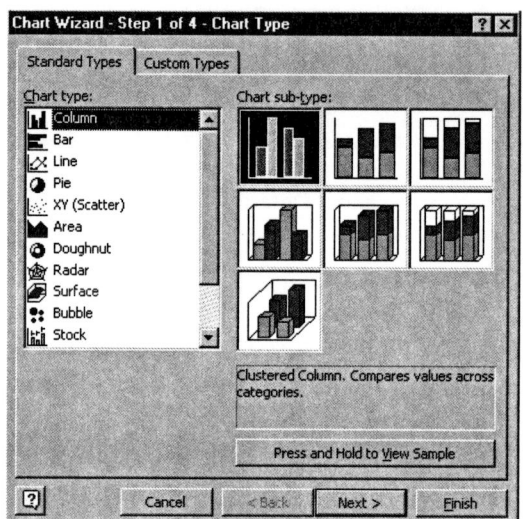

Chart Wizard button

Microsoft Access 2000 has wizards for creating tables, queries, forms and reports. For example the database window below has the command **Create report using wizard**.

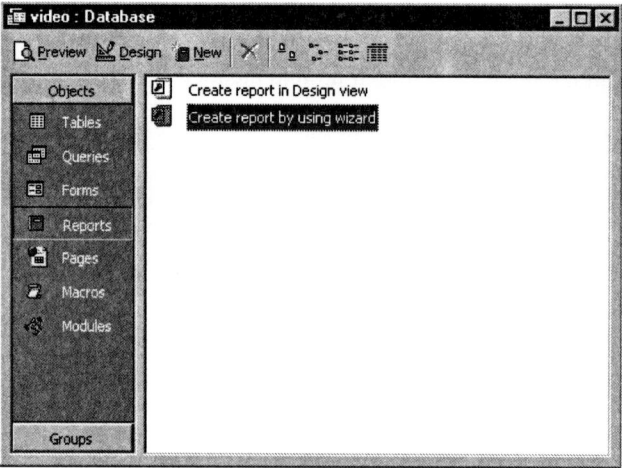

A click on this produces the first Report Wizard dialog box.

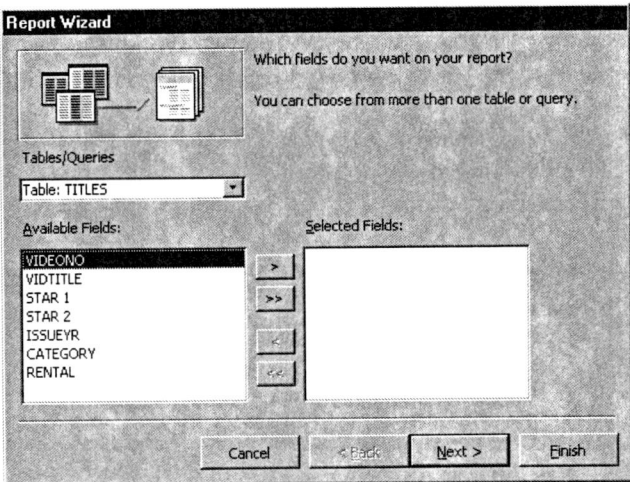

A report can be created by following the simple steps given by the wizard.

11.8 Other Automated Routines

There are many automated routines built into packages. An example is the routine that allows a user to create a chart in Word. This can be created from a table or if one is not available, it can be created from scratch.

It is possible to produce a graph in Word from a table.

To do this highlight the table and click on the **Insert** menu. Select **Object** to display the Object dialog box, select the **Create New** tab and choose **Microsoft Graph 2000 chart**. A graph of the table data will be produced.

If you do not have data in a table, the Insert Graph button will produce a sample table and graph which you can modify.

Insert Chart button

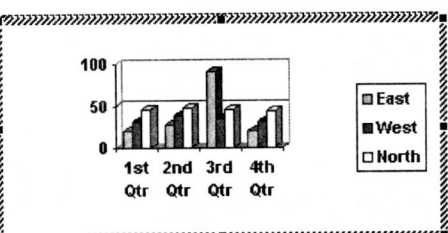

		A	B	C	D
		1st Qtr	2nd Qtr	3rd Qtr	4th Qtr
1	East	20.4	27.4	90	20.4
2	West	30.6	38.6	34.6	31.6
3	North	45.9	46.9	45	43.9

To modify a chart, activate it by double-clicking on it. Buttons on the toolbar will allow alterations to the chart.

The Chart Type button produces a selection of different charts for you to choose from.

Activity 11.3

1. Examine your word processing, spreadsheet and database software and find all the wizards that you can. The Help facility should be useful for this.

2. Write a simple guide showing how to use three of these. Include a short description of their purpose.

 **Now It's Time to Test Yourself!**

Multiple choice

1. Which printer is considered to be a page printer?

    a. ink jet printer   b. laser printer
    c. dot matrix printer

2. Which of the following printers produces the lowest quality output?

    a. ink jet printer   b. laser printer
    c. dot matrix printer

3. Which of the following is a High Level language?

    a. COBOL   b. assembler
    c. machine code   d. binary

4. Which language is the best suited to business applications?

    a. COBOL   b. FORTRAN
    c. BASIC   d. Pascal

5. Which of these components would be considered as a peripheral device?

    a. control unit   b. auxiliary storage
    c. plotter   d. arithmetic logic unit

6. If a GUI was introduced on a computer, which hardware device would be used to select the options illustrated?

    a. optical scanner   b. light pen
    c. keyboard   d. mouse

7. Which of the following types of memory is volatile?

    a. RAM   b. ROM   c. hard disk   d. auxiliary storage

8. HTML is the programming language used to:

    a. write operating systems   b. write web pages
    c. produce application packages   d. create a GUI

9. Which of the following types of software is initiated each time the computer is switched on?

    a. the operating system   b. a fourth generation language
    c. an application package   d. an assembler routine

 **Now It's Time to Test Yourself!**

Multiple choice

10. Which type of software uses mnemonics to create the instructions?

    a. machine code
    b. high level language
    c. third generation language
    d. assembler code

11. Which of the following acronyms represents a type of bar code?

    a. RAM   b. UPC   c. DASD   d. ALU

12. Which of the following is **not** an input device?

    a. a keyboard
    b. a visual display unit
    c. a light pen
    d. a character reader

Assessment
Unit 3

In this unit, you are to set up an operational ICT system to meet the needs of a user. You are to produce a description of the user requirements and a hardware and software specification.

For this unit, you must produce the following **Assessment Evidence**:

1. a description of the user requirements.

2. a hardware and software specification.

3. an operational ICT system configured to meet user needs.

The provisions for the user must include a suitable macro and template and an html program of several pages of information.

If you are successful, you will be awarded a Pass, Merit or Distinction according to the following:

Pass

To achieve a Pass your work must show:

P1 clear description of the user requirements and the basic specification for input devices, output devices, processing unit, operating system, applications software and configuration requirements.

P2 the operating system is configured appropriately, creating directory-folder structures and setting time, date, mouse, keyboard and printer drivers correctly to meet user needs. Printed copy or screen dumps appropriately annotated will show your skills.

P3 applications software is configured appropriately, setting up file locations, tool bars, backup timing, spell-checker, macro and template correctly to meet user needs. Printed copy or screen dumps appropriately annotated will show your skills.

P4 a basic design plan of the html program and create suitable text, images, sound, control buttons and hot spots to link the pages.

P5 your ability to work safely when setting up equipment, checking the accuracy of your work and keep backup copies of all files.

Merit

To achieve a Merit your work must **also** show:

M1 accurate and easy-to-read descriptions of the hardware and software with detailed definitions of input and output devices.

M2 a clear description of the html program and copies of the macro and template all clearly annotated to describe their purpose and how they work.

M3 skilled and efficient use of the operating system, application and html programming software and on-line help facilities. Annotated copies of screen prints will help to show your skills.

M4 your ability to check the accuracy of your work and corrected obvious errors.

M5 your ability to work independently to produce your work to agreed deadlines by carrying out your work plans effectively.

Distinction

To achieve a Distinction your work must **also** show:

D1 your ability to design and configure customized toolbars and keyboard actions that are well-matched to user needs and lead to significant improvements in user efficiency.

D2 several attractive, easy-to-read, easy-to-use, html pages of information that make good use of text, sound and graphic images and enable the user to move easily between the pages using button, graphic and textual hot spots.

D3 yoiur ability to produce an imaginative and accurate template and macro that clearly enable improvements in the efficiency and effectiveness of the user and facilitate high-quality output.

D4 you have edited program code to modify or correct the program (shown through annotated copies of the code before and after editing).

Chapter 12
Standard Ways of Working

When you have finished this chapter, you should be able to

- manage your work appropriately
- keep information secure
- ensure that information you produce is accurate and reliable
- work safely

12.1 Introduction

It is important that information is protected and used properly and that you should work in safety. In order that this can be achieved, a set of standard ways of working has been developed. These ways of working should be used throughout all of your ICT GNVQ work.

Information is very valuable. If information is lost or damaged, a business could collapse and people could lose their jobs.

People are very valuable. If they are injured or suffer ill health, individuals, families and businesses will suffer.

Standard ways of working have been developed to overcome problems which include:

illegal access to or copying of confidential information,
breaking copyright laws,
losing or damaging information,
generating inaccurate or poorly written information,
a poorly laid-out workplace which causes physical stress or harm to ICT operators, and
poor planning and management of work

The following sections of this chapter cover:

Managing your work,
Keeping information secure,
Accuracy and readability,
Working to commonly accepted standards and
Working safely.

12.2 Managing Your Work

A Planning Your Work

It is very important that your ICT work is planned. If not, you may not be able to complete your work in time. When you work with computers in the classroom or in a business, you will be expected to meet a deadline, i.e. you will be expected to finish your work and deliver it to a customer or teacher by a set date and possibly a set time.

Meeting a deadline is not easy. You may find that you spend too much time at the beginning of the work and have no time left to complete. To plan your work you need to break it down into smaller tasks and set dates for the completion of each. This will allow you to keep a check on how your work is progressing and it will give you advanced warning if you are slipping behind. This will give you time to make adjustments in good time, e.g. you may have to put more time into the task to allow the deadline to be met.

It may also help you to book time on a computer if you plan your work properly.

B   Organising Information

Part of the process of managing your work is concerned with organising information. When you work with computers you are working with information. You are creating information, recording information and formatting information.

It is likely that this information will need to be altered many times, so it is important that it is organised in a way that will make it easy to alter. This will include choosing a sensible file structure and using sensible filenames.

It will also involve creating file structures and document structures so that they can be easily altered and updated. The use of templates, macros and standard layouts will help in this.

C   Using Sensible Filenames

All documents should be saved regularly, even while you are creating them, so that if a document is lost, you can get a recent version back. This is called **restoring** a document.

To save a document, you have to give it a **filename**, because all documents are stored as files in the computer system.

The filename chosen should be **meaningful** so that you can find it easily in future. If a silly filename is chosen, the silliness of it will be seen later on. For instance saving a letter to a company with the filename *blobby* will not remind you later on what the letter contained or to whom it was written.

Filenames on a computer can often have only eight or less characters. This is true of files created using the DOS operating system or Windows 3.1. Windows 95 allows long filenames and are effectively as long as you want.

Filenames often have an additional set of letters added to them to show what type of file they are. These letters are called the file extension and can be up to three characters in length. The extension is separated from the file name with a *dot*. It is added to a filename to make it suitable for the wordprocessing or desktop publishing system being used.

Examples of extensions are

    .doc   showing that the file is a Word file
    .xls   showing that the file is an Excel file
    .txt   showing that the file is a text file
    .pm5 showing that the file is a Pagemaker 5.0 file

An example of a complete filename is

    newslet1.doc

which might be a newsletter produced using the Microsoft Word word processing package.

D   Keeping a Log of Your Work

Whenever you work with ICT, you will come across problems. This will be particularly true if you are working on a project or assignment. In order that you learn from your mistakes, it is important to keep a record or **log**.

This will be a computer-based or paper-based document, recording the problems you have encountered with the date and time. It will also record your solutions to the problems.

The log will be useful when you review your work.

E   Reviewing Your Work

Part of the process of managing your work is the process of reviewing it. It is important that you look regularly at the work you have produced to see that it matches what you expected. If you are working for a customer, you will need to check your work against the expectations of the customer.

This process will enable you to use your log to consider any problems that you have met and how you overcame them. It will also enable you to change, where necessary, the way you do your work. This will bring about improvements in your approach and the work itself.

The plan that you set yourself will involve not only the tasks and deadlines but also the stages at which you think that a review would be useful.

At the very end of your work, you should make a review of the whole project so that you will be better able to prepare and carry out the next.

12.3 Keeping Information Secure

A   Security

Information must be secure because it plays an all important part in any business. In fact, if data is corrupt and no security measures are in place then the majority of firms will go out of business.

What dangers are there to prevent data security?

Natural Disasters

Floods, fires, earthquakes and other natural disasters can, as with any other possession, damage or destroy data.   An electricity cut or any other interruption to supply could cause data to be lost. Laptop computers can suffer injury in transport or with battery break down.

Human Error

As no one is perfect, human errors can destroy or greatly damage data. This can be caused by accidentally deleting important files or parts of files or incorrectly opening and saving documents from different packages. This can cause corruption of data.

People can forget to save files before exiting a system.

They might not exit the program correctly, which may make data unreadable when re-opening that file.

Deliberate Destruction - Computer Crime

From upset employees to espionage from competitors, deliberate faults can be installed in data handling systems. There are bugs and viruses that cause enormous damage. An example is one that formats discs, wiping out existing data. Incorrect data can be deliberately entered, which would cause havoc in a business, especially anything to do with finance.

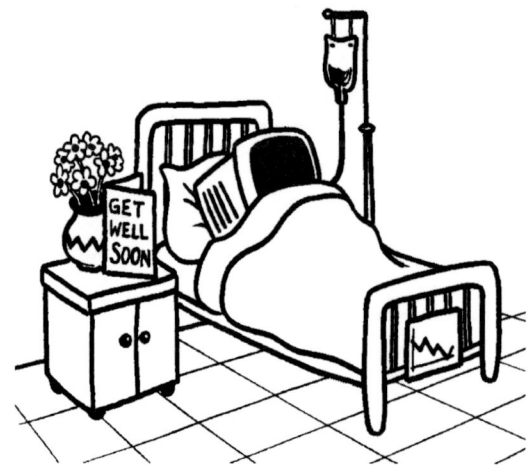

B Maintaining Security

Backup

A backup is a copy of data and should be kept separately from its original. It is imperative that all files be backed up on a regular basis. The backup should be stored on a separate medium, such as tape or floppy disc. The backups should also be stored in another location; another building, another room. If this is not possible, the backups should be stored in fire-proof safes.

A well managed system will have a good backup procedure in place. The backing up of files should be done on a set day, at a set time to ensure that the routine is implemented correctly. It is far from the most exciting of jobs to back up a computer system but it is absolutely vital if the organisation is to rely on the system.

How often the organisation needs to back up data files will obviously depend on the type of data being held. There is a standard procedure for backing up and this is often referred to as the **grandfather, father and son**, i.e. generations of files. This means that three versions of files will be held; the **son** which is the current file will be held on immediate storage while the **father and grandfather,** earlier versions of the files, will be stored in a fire-proof, flood-proof safe.

Regular Saving

At a certain point, when keying in data, either at a page break in wordprocessing or after a limited amount of time, files should be saved. If there should then be a power cut or other interruption in electrical supply, the data lost would be minimal, a page or screen full, rather than a day's worth of input.

Some systems have automatic backups, whereby the software continually saves the data. Some software automatically makes backup copies of files.

Virus Checks

Software is now available for checking for viruses on a hard or floppy disc. This procedure can be built into the booting of the machine, guaranteeing that the check scans the hard disc every time that the machine is turned on or re-booted. Instructions would have to be keyed in at the prompt to scan floppy discs for viruses.

C Copyright

Most books, documents, music and software is copyright. This means that you have to get permission if you want the **right** to **copy** it and permssion may not be granted. This makes copying without permission an illegal offence.

Within software, the name of the person or organisation who originally bought it will be evident on screen. Some software is bought with a network licence, or licence for an agreed number of terminals. Some software has special concessions for education, either unlimited within the campus, or an abridged edition, limiting the amount of records and facilities. Some software comes with programmed obstacles, making it very difficult to copy it.

Documents and information produced by businesses are also copyright. Documents will carry the copyright symbol.

The Copyright Symbol

D   Confidentiality

It is important to protect the confidentiality of information. Businesses own information and they do not want other businesses to gain access to it. Individuals have information that they do not wish to reveal to others, e.g. doctor's patients' records are confidential.

There is much information that is available openly to all who wish to access it. For instance, the internet is full of it. But where the availablity of information would do damage to an individual, a business or society, it should be protected.

Governments and organisations can hide behind confidentiality claims to hide information that should be available openly and an important debate is taking place currently on the freedom of information.

12.4   Accuracy and Readability

When you are producing documents, it is important that they are easy to read. If not, the reader will struggle to follow the document, may get annoyed and may stop trying to read it. This could be a disaster for you. You may have produced a letter applying for a job, in which case you are likely not to get the job. You may have produced a document which you hoped to sell, such as a magazine, and your sales may be poor. Documents are produced to be read and if they cannot be read they have failed.

Word processing software provides the facility to help the user to produce readable documents. It will provide a spell-checker, which is a piece of software which checks each word in a document and if it does not recognise the word as being spelt correctly, will tell you so and will offer you some correctly-spelt alternative words.

Sometimes it will not recognise a correctly spelt word, and you do not have to accept the suggestions. People's names and addresses often provide this type of difficulty.

Some spell-checkers will only check a document when you ask it to and others will check each word as you type it.

Word processors also have grammar checkers. They look at the way you have written your sentences and will offer alternatives. They will, for instance, check that the each sentence starts with a capital letter, ends with a full stop, and has a subject and verb that agree.

As well as using computer software to check documents, you will have to be able to proof-read them. This is the difficult process of reading a document carefully for errors and then marking them up for correction using standard symbols.

12.5 Organisations and Standard Formats

Commercial organisations use many documents. These include business letters, memoranda, reports, newsletters, invoices, minutes and agendas. In order to project the image of their organisation they develop a **corporate image**. This is created by creating all their documents with the same style and layout and using the same company logo or trade mark on each. This is called a **corporate style** or **house style**. In fact, it is more likely to be the logo that is recognised by the public. This means that when a member of the public or a customer sees a document, they know from its style which organisation it is. If you look around you, will see many examples of this. The Virgin range of companies use a written version of their name on all their materials and advertisements which is instantly recognised by the public. Tesco and Sainsbury have names that are recognised by style as do many other high street shops.

A corporate style is chosen to ensure that information is simply presented and creates an image that provides good publicity.

Organisations like to project a recognisable corporate image to the public and like to win loyalty from the public for their goods and services. They aim for their name and logo to be associated with their goods and services.

A corporate style will include standard document layouts, so that memos, letters, minutes and other documents will have the same style, including logos and text and number styles.

You will need to be able to produce documents with a standard style and learn to proof read them using correction symbols such as.

Symbol	Explanation
lc	Lower case - small letters
uc or CAPS	Upper case - capital letters
☐	Insert full stop
#	Insert space
NP	Insert new paragraph
Run on	No new paragraph required. Carry straight on
λ	Insert letter or words
~~Strike out~~	Delete or take out
Stet	Let it stand, i.e. ignore the correction made

12.6 Working Safely

The environment for those working with ICT is relatively safe, but there are hazards and many people suffer physical damage using computers over a long period of time. It is important to avoid problems arising from bad posture, long periods in front of the screen and poor layout of furniture and equipment.

The Health and Safety at Work Act of 1974 provides regulations and codes of practice for those at work. The requirements include the following:

* lighting and ventilation must be satisfactory,
* room temperature must be at least 16°C, after the first hour,
* offices, furniture etc. must be kept in a clean condition,
* sanitation, cloakroom, first aid and fresh water facilities must be provided,
* employees' working space must not be overcrowded,
* employers must comply with local authority fire regulations,
* suitable chairs must be provided,
* regular inspection of machines should take place,
* no trailing wires or cables should be present,
* filing cabinets should not be top heavy and
* carpets should not be frayed.

Schools and Colleges have to adhere to the Health and Safety at Work Act. In organisations, both employers and employees have responsibility in law to ensure a safe and healthy working environment.

You should have a comfortable working position at your computer and you should not be looking at the screen for long periods of time - it is suggested that you take a break from the computer every two hours.

Index

A
Accuracy, 126
Absolute cell reference, 66
Address, 42
Advertisement, 13
Agenda, 12, 16, 21
Alignment, 30
Application software, 93, 96
    configuration, 104
    testing, 105
    types, 101
Arithmetic/logical unit, 87
Assembly language, 96
Automated routines, 112, 115
Auxiliary storage, 89

B
Backup, 125
Back-up storage devices, 92
Bar code reader, 83
Batch files, 112
Batch program, 94
Bold text, 26
Borders, 32
Bullets, 8, 32
Business
    card, 16
    letter, 9, 16, 20
Byte, 89

C
Cache memory, 88
Calculations, 53
Case, 30
CD Rom, 91
Cell, 52, 66
    format, 67
    reference, 52, 66
Central processing unit, 80, 87
Charts, 16, 31, 72
Clip Art, 111
COBOL, 97
Columns, 33
Commercial documents, 20
    agenda, 21
    business letter, 20
    memorandum, 21
    minutes, 22
    newsletter, 21
    purchasing documents, 22
    sales documents, 22
    report, 21
Confidentiality, 126
Commercial software, 98

C (cont.)
Compact disk, 91
Compiler, 97
Computer programming, 107
Contents, 44
Control unit, 83
Copyright, 125

D
Data, 41
    duplication, 59
    integrity, 59
    types, 59
Database, 44, 49, 102
    construction, 60
    design, 59
        information needs, 59
        user needs, 59
    hypertext, 49
    methods, 57
    number-structured, 51
    record-structured, 50
    relational, 50
    table, 50
Database terms, 57
    field, 57
    field data types, 59
    field length, 58
    field name, 58
    foreign key, 58
    primary key, 58
    record, 57
Delivery note, 22
Design
    database, 57
    implementation, 54
Desktop, 99
Desk top publishing, 102
Digital versatile disk, 91
Digitiser, 83
Directory, 94
Disk, 86
    compact, 91
    DVD, 91
    hard, 90
    floppy, 90
Document
    layout, 16
        fonts, 19
        headers and footers, 18
        line spacing, 19
        margins, 17
        page orientation, 17
        paragraph format, 17

D (cont.)
Document
   layout (cont.)
      paper size, 17
   types, 16
DVD, 91

E
E-mail, 104

F
Field, 57
   length, 58
   name, 58
File, 94, 100
   maintenance, 94
Filenames, 122
Floppydisk, 90
Folder, 94, 100
Fonts, 19, 30
   sizes, 30
Footers, 18
Foreign key, 58
Formal letter, 11
Formal invitation, 14
Format, 17
Forms, 14
Formula, 48, 55, 74
FORTRAN, 97
Fourth generation languages, 97
Front End, 94
Function, 48, 55

G
Gigabyte, 89
Graphics, 31, 103
Graphics user interface, 95
Graphs, 16, 31
GUI, 91

H
Hard disk, 90
Hardware, 79
Headers, 18
Headings, 29
High level language, 97
HTML programming, 108
Hypertext database, 49

I
ICT system, 79
Indexes, 33
Information, 41
   finding, 46
   sources, 41
   structure, 42
   types, 15, 48

I (cont.)
Information handling systems, 53
   data and information requirements, 54
   design, 53
   input requirements, 55
   output requirements, 53
   software requiremnts, 53
Input devices 81
   bar code reader, 83
   digitiser, 83
   digital camera, 83
   joystick, 84
   keyboard, 81
   microphone, 83
   mouse, 82
   scanner, 83
   tracker ball, 82
Interpreter, 97
Invoice, 22
Italic text, 26
Itineraries, 16

J
Job application, 11
Joystick, 84
Justification, 30

K
Keyboard, 81
Keys, 56
   foreign, 56
   primary, 56
Kilobyte, 89

L
Language style, 9
Letter, 43
Line graphs, 70
Line spacing, 19
Log, 39
Logical operator, 48
Logical value, 48
Loud Speaker, 86
Low level language, 96
Lower case, 30

M
Machine language, 96
Machine oriented, 96
Macro programming, 111
Main storage, 88
Managing your work, 121
   organising information, 122
   planning, 121
   reviewing, 123
Margins, 17

M (cont.)
Megabyte, 89
Memorandum, 21
Memory map, 96
Minutes, 12, 16, 22
Mnemonic, 96
Mouse, 82, 100

N
Newsletters, 16, 21
Numbering, 9, 32
Numbers, 15, 44, 48
Number-structured database, 51

O
Operating system, 94
   configuration, 99
   testing, 105
Order, 22
Output devices, 84
   loudspeaker, 86
   plotter, 86
   printer, 84

P
Page orientation, 17
Paper size, 17
Paragraph format, 17
Passwords, 101
Plotter, 86
Positioning, 19
Presentation
   styles, 7
   techniques, 25
Primary key, 58
Printer, 84
   dot matrix, 84
   ink jet, 85
   laser, 85
Processor
   types, 89
Programming, 107
   HMTL, 108
Programming language, 96

R
Random access memory, 88
RAM, 88
Readability, 126
Read only memory, 88
Record, 44, 57
Record-structured database, 50
Relational database, 50
   management system, 51, 60

R (cont.)
Relational operator, 47
Relative cell reference, 64
Reports, 16, 21
ROM, 88

S
Safety, 128
Scanner, 83
Searching, 47, 53
   using logical operators, 45
   using relational operators, 45
Search machines, 44
Security, 124
Selecting, 53
Shading, 32
Software, 79, 93
   applications, 93, 96
   system, 93
   tools, 97
Sorting, 47, 45, 53
Source of information, 42
Special symbols, 33
Spreadsheet, 49, 63, 103
   if..then..else, 67
   methods, 65
   terms, 65
     cell, 66
      format, 67
     cell reference, 66
      absolute, 66
      relative, 66
     formula, 66
     function, 66
Standard Formats, 127
Storage capacity, 89
Structure of Information, 40
Subscript, 29
Superscript, 29
System prompt, 90
System software, 89

T
Tab, 28
Tables, 14, 15, 27, 44, 61
Template, 22, 26
Terabyte, 89
Text, 15, 48
Titles, 29
Tracker ball, 82
Types of information, 46
   date/time, 46
   formula, 46
   function, 46
   logical, 46
   number, 46
   text, 46

U
Upper case, 30
User needs, 59

V
Virus
 anti-virus checks, 101, 125

W
Web page
 design, 110
 publishing, 109
What-if, 55, 68
White space, 26
Wizards, 114
Word processing, 101
Writing styles, 7
 attracting attention, 7
 explaining details, 9
 meeting the needs of the user, 7
 setting out facts clearly, 8
 summarising information, 9